Praise for *Are You Somebody?*

"One of the most perfectly observed portraits of female loneliness I've ever come across—with more genuine, painful candor in it than all the modish, scandalous confessions of recent years put together."
—Zoë Heller, *The New York Times*

"Funny, plainspoken, heartfelt . . . Though her memoir is more fascinating on subjects other than love, it is to love that O'Faolain returns again and again throughout the book."
—Lynn Freed, *Elle*

"A remarkable memoir, poignant, truthful, and imparting that quiet wisdom which suffering brings."
—Edna O'Brien

"[An] evocative memoir."
—*People* magazine

"[A] searing, unsentimental book."
—Maureen Dezell, *The Boston Globe*

"An extraordinary, powerful memoir. It is beautifully written, with an honesty that is both sensitive and stark. Writing about herself, Nuala O'Faolain has also written about Ireland. It is a cruel, wounded place—and this book has become an important part of the cure."
—Roddy Doyle

"[A] brilliant, literary memoir."
—Sabina Lawlor Clarke, *The Philadelphia Inquirer*

"Likely to become a classic of Irish autobiography."
—Colm Tóibín, *The Times Literary Supplement* (London)

"I kept marveling at how such pain and grief, sorrow and anger and loss could make such joyful reading."
—Terry Doran, *The Buffalo News*

ARE YOU SOMEBODY?

The Accidental Memoir
of a Dublin Woman

N U A L A   O ' F A O L A I N

AN OWL BOOK
HENRY HOLT AND COMPANY • NEW YORK

Henry Holt and Company, Inc.
Publishers since 1866
115 West 18th Street
New York, New York 10011

Henry Holt® is a registered
trademark of Henry Holt and Company, Inc.

Published in Canada by Fitzhenry & Whiteside Ltd.,
195 Allstate Parkway, Markham, Ontario L3R 4T8.

Library of Congress Cataloging-in-Publication Data
O'Faolain, Nuala.
Are you somebody?: the accidental memoir of a Dublin
woman / Nuala O'Faolain.
          p.   cm.
Originally published: Dublin: New Island Books, © 1996.
Includes columns originally published in the Irish Times.
ISBN 0-8050-5664-5
1. O'Faolain, Nuala.   2. Women journalists—Ireland—
               Biography.   I. Title
PN5146.039A3   1998   97-29725
070'.92—dc21   CIP
[B]

Henry Holt books are available for special promotions and
premiums. For details contact: Director, Special Markets.

First published in hardcover in 1998 by
Henry Holt and Company, Inc.

First Owl Books Edition 1999

Designed by Michelle McMillian

Printed in the United States of America
All first editions are printed on acid-free paper. ∞

7 9 10 8 6

An extension of this copyright appears on page 217.

ARE YOU SOMEBODY?

INTRODUCTION

I was born in a Dublin that was much more like something from an earlier century than like the present day. I was one of nine children, when nine was not even thought of as a big family, among the teeming, penniless, anonymous Irish of the day. I was typical: a nobody, who came of an unrecorded line of nobodies. In a conservative Catholic country, which feared sexuality and forbade me even information about my body, I could expect difficulty in getting through my life as a girl and a woman. But at least—it would have been assumed—I wouldn't have the burden of having to earn a good wage. Eventually some man would marry me and keep me.

But there are no typical people. And places don't stay the same. The world changed around Ireland, and even Ireland changed, and I was to be both an agent of change and a beneficiary of it. I didn't see that, until I wrote out my story. I was immured in the experience of my own life. Most of the time I just went blindly from day to day, and though what I was doing must have looked ordinary enough—growing up in the countryside, getting through school, falling in love, discovering lust, learning, working, travelling, moving in and out of health and happiness—to myself I was usually barely hanging on. I never stood back and looked at myself and what I was doing. I didn't value myself enough—take myself seriously enough—to reflect even privately on whether my existence had any pattern, any meaning. I took it for granted that like most of the billions of people who are born and die on this planet I was just an accident. There was no reason for me.

Yet my life burned inside me. Even such as it was, it was the only record of me, and it was my only creation, and something in me would not accept that it was insignificant. Something in me must have been waiting to stand up and demand to be counted. Because eventually, when I was presented with an opportunity to talk about myself, I grasped at it. I'm on my own anyway, I thought. What have I to lose? But I needed to speak, too. I needed to howl.

What happened was that in my forties, back in the Dublin of my birth, I began working for the most respected newspaper in the country—*The Irish Times*—as an opinion columnist. This was a wonderful job to have, and a quite unexpected one. The very idea of an Irishwoman opinion columnist would have been unthinkable for most of my life. The columns were usually about politics or social questions or moments in popular culture—they weren't personal at all. They used a confident, public voice. My readers probably thought I was as confident as that all the time, but I knew the truth. My private life was solitary. My private voice was apologetic. In terms of national influence I mattered, in Ireland. But I possessed nothing of what has traditionally mattered to women and what had mattered to me during most of my life. I had no lover, no child. It seemed to me that I had nothing to look back on but failure.

But when I'd been writing my columns for ten years or so, a publisher came to me and asked whether he could put some of them together in book form. I said that was fine. No one would track my work through the back numbers of the newspaper, but a book gets around. It might be the only thing to read in a trekker's hut in Nepal. It would be catalogued in the National Library. It would be there for my grandniece, who is only a baby now. But I wasn't interested in the old columns. I was interested in what I would say in the personal introduction I'd promised to write.

What would I say about myself, the person who *wrote* the columns? Now that I had the opportunity, how would I introduce myself?

I'm fairly well known in Ireland. I've been on television a lot, and there's a photo of me in the paper, at the top of my column. But I'm no star. People have to look at me twice or three times to put a name on me. Sometimes when I'm drinking in a lounge bar, a group of women, say, across the room, may look at me and send one of their number over to me, or when I'm in the grocery store someone who has just passed me by turns back and comes right up to me and scrutinises my face. "Are you somebody?" they ask. Well—am I somebody? I'm not anybody in terms of the world, but then, who decides what a somebody is? How is a somebody made? I've never done anything remarkable; neither have most people. Yet most people, like me, feel remarkable. That self-importance welled up inside me. I had the desire to give an account of my life. I was finished with furtiveness. I sat down to write the introduction, and I summoned my pride. I turned it into a memoir.

I imagined the hostile response I'd get in my little Irish world. "Who does she think she is?" I could hear the reviewers saying. But it turned out not to be like that at all. The world my story went out to turned out to be much, much bigger than I'd ever thought. And it turned out to be full of people who knew me, who were sisters and brothers although we had never met, who were there to welcome me coming out of the shadows, and who wanted to throw off the shadows that obscured their own lives, too. My small voice was answered by a rich chorus of voices: my voice, which had once been mute! Of all the places where my story might start, even, it started itself at a point in my life when I could not speak at all. . . .

1

When I was in my early thirties and entering a bad period of my life, I was living in London on my own, working as a television producer with the BBC. The man who had absorbed me for ten years, and whom I had once been going to marry, had finally left. I came home one day to the flat in Islington, and there was a note on the table saying *Back Tuesday*. I knew he wouldn't come back, and he didn't. I didn't really want him to. We were exhausted. But still, I didn't know what to do. I used to sit in my chair every night and read and drink a lot of cheap white wine. I'd say "hello" to the fridge when its motor turned itself on. One New Year's Eve I wished the announcer on Radio Three "A Happy New Year to you, too." I was very depressed. I asked the doctor to send me to a psychiatrist.

The psychiatrist was in an office in a hospital. "Well, now, let's get your name right to begin with," he said cheerfully. "What is your name?" "My name is . . . my name is . . ." I could not say my name. I cried, as from an ocean of tears, for the rest of the hour. My self was too sorrowful to speak. And I was in the wrong place, in England. My name was a burden to me.

Not that the psychiatrist saw it like that. I only went to him once more, but I did manage to get out a bit about my background and about the way I was living. Eventually he said something that lifted a corner of the fog of unconsciousness. "You are going to great trouble," he said, "and flying in the face of the facts of your life, to re-create your mother's life." Once he said this, I could see it was true. Mammy sat in her chair in a flat in Dublin and read and drank. Before she sat in the chair she was in bed. She might venture shakily down to the pub. Then she would totter home and sit in her chair. Then she went to bed. She had had to work the treadmill of feeding and clothing and cleaning child after child for decades. Now all but one of the nine had gone. My father had moved himself and her and that last one to a flat, and she sat there. She had the money he gave her (never enough to slake her anxieties). She had nothing to do, and there was nothing she wanted to do, except drink and read.

And there was I—half her age, not dependent on anyone, not tired or trapped, with an interesting, well-paid job, with freedom and health and occasional good looks. Yet I was loyally re-creating her wasteland around myself.

One of the stories of my life has been the working out in it of her powerful and damaging example—in everything. Nothing matters except passion, she indicated. It was what had mattered to her, and she more or less sustained a myth of passionate happiness for the first ten years of her marriage. She didn't value any other kind of relationship. She wasn't interested in friendship. If she had thoughts or ideas, she never mentioned them. She was more like a shy animal on the outskirts of the human settlement than a person within it. She read all the time, not to feed reflection but as part of her utter determination to avoid reflection.

What made her? Her father—my grandad—wrote his memoirs, a few pages in pencil, in a lined copybook. He was one of fourteen children on a smallholding, and perhaps because, like his brothers and sisters, he had had to emigrate when he was a boy and there was never a family again, he remembered his childhood home with an abundance of sentiment. "I will try and give you a typical family scene as I saw it in the beginning of the 1890s," he wrote:

Father would enter the kitchen after dark and would start making and mending—a chair, a basket, or some harness. He would always sing at his work, he having a great variety of songs in both English and Irish. The babies would be asleep and the next elders would have their feet washed in a wooden vessel, then follow. After the rosary was said the next elders would retire. Mother would be putting the last thread in her needle. An oil lamp hung before the window and a turf fire in the hearth would be supplemented by a piece of bog deal which cast a light on the dresser so that the jugs and other ware would gleam as if alight. Sometimes, when not engaged in work, Father would pull down the weekly paper and read aloud, mostly the political news—stopping now and then to put his own interpretation on it. Mother, near at hand, would be an eager listener.

My mother, the granddaughter of this ideal pair, was anything but an eager listener. I don't know what happened, down the generations. I don't suppose that history explains it—that the individual person comes out of a vessel into which two jugs called Heredity and Environment have been poured. But perhaps emigration did something to the relationship between women and children. Children were toughened early, sent out into the world with their cardboard suitcases—one minute warm in the tribe, the next minute walking down the steps of some distant railway station into a world they must handle on their own. Under the surface competence, they must have been infantile. Somewhere in the years that fed down into my mother, there were too many children and too few resources. She was the most motherless of women, herself. Her own mother, in the little account anyone ever gave of her, was angry and energetic, running a tailoress operation in the front room of the red-brick terraced house in Clonliffe Road in Dublin, sewing shrouds late at night for the dead of the parish. Tuberculosis makes you feverish, and she was slowly dying of TB. "She threw a red-hot iron at me," was all my mother ever said—sulkily—about her. "She said I always had my head stuck in a book." But then, one child had already died. One grown-up daughter was dying of TB along with the mother. There were seven more being reared for emigration. It was an ordinary respectable Irish household of the time. The woman of the house never went out, never had money, never stopped having children. My own mother held herself at arm's length from this reality. She grew up with no skills. She didn't know how to make small-talk or cook a breakfast or tie up a parcel or name a tree or flower.

When I knew my grandfather he had long been a widower. He dreamt of champion greyhounds and hobbled up Clonliffe Road to a public bench, where he talked slowly with other patriarchs, other countrymen displaced. I didn't know why my mother feared him. He ate bull's-eyes and read *The Saint* thrillers. He would say to me from his frowsty bed, "Hand me over those trousers." He'd fumble in the pocket and give me pennies. He sat on the upright chair to put on his long johns, and his penis was like some purply barnacled mineral thing, found on the seabed. He expected his tea and bread-and-butter brought to his chair. He would certainly have denied that the fact that three of his children were ferocious alcoholics had anything to do with him. No one takes responsibility for the big Irish families that in generation after generation are ravaged by alcoholism.

My mother didn't want anything to do with child-rearing or housework. But she had to do it. Because she fell in love with my father, and they married, she was condemned to spend her life as a mother and a homemaker. She was in the wrong job. Sometimes I meet women who remind me of her when I stay in bed-and-breakfasts around the country. They throw sugar on the fire, to get it to light, and wipe surfaces with an old rag that smells, and they are forever sending children to the shops.

They question me, half censorious, half wistful: "And did you never want to get married yourself?"

The one thing my mother knew definitely existed was her body. She was sent home from convent boarding-school because of dancing too close to the girl she adored. She was baffled by the punishment, never having heard of lesbianism. I remember a Henry Green novel which passed through the house when I was a child, whose cover had a sketch of girls in white dresses waltzing together in the half-dark. Mammy blossomed for a moment, seeing it. "That's exactly what it was like! In the big hall in school! The night I danced with her!" Decades later, not long before my mother died, a bright-eyed middle-aged lady came up to me at a reception. It was in the offices of the then Council for the Status of Women, as it happens. "How is your mother?" she asked. She, it turned out, was the other girl, the love-object. I didn't dare ask her what had really happened. Anyway, by then what mattered was the contrast between this spry woman, obviously someone who knew what status was, and the wreck of my poor innocent and ignorant mother, out in the little flat, making her way through days of shakiness and gagged-on gin, while her husband blandly went about his business and the last of her children—a schoolgirl, then—brought herself up.

This was where grand passion had left her.

Her foremothers knew how the tribe expected women to behave and how it would protect them in return. But when my grandfather came back from exile in London to work in the General Post Office in Dublin around 1910, and the link with Kerry was broken, no one belonged to a tribe. My mother was on her own. But without hope of independence. Nowadays she could have stayed in the civil service, even after she became pregnant. But 1940s Ireland was a living tomb for women.

For men like my father, out and about in Dublin, the opposite was true. Broadcasting and journalism were beginning to open up. He had begun as a teacher, in the 1930s, and if he had stayed in teaching—coming home in the afternoons every day, and free in the summer—his children would have had a wonderful father. But he had many gifts and ambitions: He was a traveller in Europe in the summers, and a linguist and a sportsman, and a happy, proud patriot. And handsome as anything.

There are photos of himself and my mother on the beach at Ballybunnion, all white teeth and strong limbs. She was blissfully happy with how he made her feel about herself. They were mad about each other from the start. They hiked over Howth Head and Bray Head and up the Dublin mountains and made love in the heather. He bought her a hot port one chilly evening, her first drink ever. They married very early on a January morning because my sister Grainne was a little bump under Mammy's dress. The Second World War started. He joined the Irish Defence Forces in 1939 and loved army life. Not long after my mother was pregnant again; he cycled up from the Curragh Camp to the Rotunda Hospital to greet me. But I spent my infancy in Donegal, because the Army brought my father there. The first few pages of a letter from him to my mother arranging the move survive. She was pregnant again.

"*A chroidhe dhil*," he begins. For years I could not read this letter. "Beloved heart," when they ended so badly! He is writing from Fort Dunree, up on the Inishowen peninsula. He has found a little house for the family—he encloses a sketch—and continues:

> For Grainne and Nuala there is quiet, air, sun and sea, chickens for Grainne not to mention an occasional *bó*. For you there are these things, plus me, plus an odd weekend trip to Derry and evenings in Buncrana. As regards books, Father Dolan has a pile of great stuff, which I know he will lend to you. There are other things—eggs, milk, potatoes straight from their cradles. And even though coal will play second-fiddle to turf, there will be no pennies in the gas. The reek is about twenty yards of a walk— no trouble to an enthusiastic husband. . . . Today is Wednesday—and I find I will not be paid my 6/2d until tomorrow—but

I am borrowing money for a stamp. Almost a week now since I saw you last and it feels like a month. I am counting the days till we all get together again in the lovely sunshine. Today the sun shone for twelve hours, and all the day, from 9 a.m. till 6 p.m., I was on duty on a grass-topped cliff, giving a hand to recruits who were engaged in rifle practice.

His letter is overtaken by one from her. He went on:

Your letters usually make me feel bloody awful, but this one was not too bad! I notice that I have influenced you to the extent that you say "a bit difficult" when you mean "quite desperate." Good Girl.

"Ah so!" I say. "She was already provoking him with her despair." But then—three children in four years! The end of the letter is missing, so the taboo on a parent's intimate life was not breached, if there were intimacies there.

He treats my mother as a partner in this letter. He's doing freelance journalism, and she's helping him. But when I knew them, he went out; she stayed home. Nobody treated her as a partner. When she died, a few years after him, this letter was found in the old tin biscuit box that was her only possession, apart from clothes. She didn't own a single thing in the little flat—not a book, not a record. In the biscuit tin there were the scrawled pages of book reviews she had written, in pencil and ballpoint pen. They had moved house at least a dozen times. She had gone to great trouble, then, to keep this letter and the reviews. A few of her book reviews were published in the paper. That was the only money she ever earned for herself, apart from the children's allowance. That was what she talked about—the money. But it wasn't for the money that she kept the crumpled drafts in the biscuit tin, when she had nothing else. She could have been respected, if things had been different. She could have done something other than be the drudge she was.

13

. . .

It seems that very early in the marriage she was overwhelmed. She foundered, and either he didn't see it or he saw it but couldn't help. It must have happened quickly. A woman who worked for my parents when they came back from Donegal told me Grainne and I were always identically dressed in pretty clothes. What I remember, from only three or four years later, is the teacher in Miss Ahern's school in Malahide calling me in to her office and fingering my dirty cardigan. "Couldn't your mother find anything better to send you to school in?"

She was to have thirteen pregnancies altogether: nine living children. She never had enough money. She did her best for years. She made crabapple jam. She gave us jam sandwiches and a milk-of-magnesia bottle full of milk for our picnic. She bought us Wellington boots for the winter. She fine-combed our hair, us kneeling before her, bent into the newspaper on her lap. Think of all the clothes she must have bought, washed, dried, sorted out, put on our backs. . . . We lived in a rented bungalow meant for a farm labourer, on a gentry estate in north County Dublin. The bungalow was surrounded by fields with ditches and hawthorn hedges in what was an isolated landscape, then. The railway line from Dublin passed the other side of a turnip field. Sometimes Daddy jumped from the train and rolled down the embankment as a shortcut home. But he began not to come home. He was a clerk in the Irish Tourist Board after the Army, but then he began to get work in Radio Éireann, and to get jobs—like doing the commentary on the "Radio Train" to Killarney—that took him away. His life became more exciting all the time. He brought his joie de vivre home with him when he came striding across the field to where we were playing—making "houses" and "shops" from stones and mud—around the house. We would hear the bright whistle of *"Beidh Aonach Amárach"* or some other Irish tune, and we'd run to jump up on the fence to see him. "Daddy's home! He's home!"

Her life got harder. The Calor gas cylinder under the two rings she cooked on would run out, and she had no phone or transport. She washed clothes in the bath, with yellow soap and a washboard. We were no consolation. Once, when my father had gone down the country on a job, she broke the unwritten rules by daringly going into Dublin, to Kingsbridge station, and surprising him by being at the barrier when he got off the train. He was with people. He leaned down to aim a kiss at her cheek before hurrying off with them. "He didn't even take the cigarette out of his mouth," she told me, not once but over and over again, in years to come.

I imagine her making her lonely way back to us children. She was still in her twenties. She would have taken the bus out to the terminus, then walked out past the last streetlamp, then down the dark country road to the estate's gate-lodge, then ducked under a fence and followed the path we'd worn in the tussocky field across to the bungalow. . . . Nothing there but children. Another time—it was late at night, but I was awake in my bed because I was counting my Communion money for the twentieth time—I heard him come in and then I heard her shrieking, "That's not my lipstick!" That would have been near the end of the ten perfect years she always claimed they had. Around then, one of his women (she had a daughter by him that she called Nuala, ambiguously enough) came out to our place to bargain with my mother. This woman had money. She offered Mammy a large allowance to let him go with her to Australia. I remember this woman leaving hurriedly along the path through the field, and my father running after her, and my mother running after him, crying. Then Mammy fell in a heap in the grass. It was a summer's day, and the cattle were already sitting quietly around the field. She was a rounded shape in the grass, like a small cow.

Soon after, my mother had an affair with my father's friend, though she didn't like him at all. What other weapon did she have? To make my father notice? But the men took no notice of her. They absorbed her protest; it didn't cause a ripple between them. So then she had nothing left to protest with.

Unhappiness settled on her gradually. She was gauche. She had a more charming sister who sometimes came home from abroad and brought fun into our house. This aunt used to seek our company. I learnt to believe that she enjoyed being with us. She was with us when we were packed into a bulging Ford Prefect with just clothes and dishes. We had been evicted from the bungalow and ended up living in a small town, further away from Dublin.

It was in that grey little town that my mother began to drink by herself. She went out to the pub in the evening. She began to look around to see where there might be chemist shops where she could get what she wanted to help her to diet. We were living then in a crumbling rectory with lovely drawing rooms and an overgrown garden with a dog's graveyard behind the apple trees, and stone-flagged sculleries full of spiders. The first year we were there, the suave American voice of Perry Como was everywhere, singing "Don't let the stars get in your eyes, don't let the moon make you cry...." And Daddy was in America, too. At Christmas, he brought Mammy home a figure-hugging black dress. "I like you thin," he said. By now my father had turned into a journalist under the name Terry O'Sullivan. He went away around the country five days a week, now, writing for the *Sunday Press*. Her sister, who was more fun than she was, sometimes went with him. There was no question of my mother going; she had seven children in the house.

"I like you thin." That edict of his echoed in my life, too, and in some of my brothers' and sisters' lives. I went around the chemist shops for my mother. I internalised her panic at not being able to sleep. I was addicted to sleeping tablets for years. It is hard for children to withhold assent from their mother—to stand far enough apart to judge that what she is doing is not part of nature.

I once asked my friend, the broadcaster and writer Sean Mac Réamoinn, who knew my father and mother in the 1950s, what class we belonged to. We had very little money, and home was bleak, compared to the homes of our school friends. But my mother read all the time, and my father taught us the words of German songs, and we played extracts from *Swan*

Lake on the gramophone, and we put on plays, whereas the other families we knew did not do those things. "Were we working class?" I asked
him. "Because we certainly weren't middle class." "What you were was
bohemian," he said.

But bohemians *care* about music or literature or art. My parents had
no real resource there, any more than they had positive values—actually
believed in the merit of individual freedom or anything else. The values
of their own parents seemed to have no meaning for them. They did not
care about respectability—they didn't "know their place." Mammy
would send me up the field to the big Georgian house where the landlady
lived, with the rent. She hated paying the rent. "Throw it at her!" she'd
snarl at me. They were not practising Catholics, either. We had to go to
Mass, certainly. But they didn't. Whatever the people they came from
had lived by just fell away in their generation. But they didn't have other
values, to replace what they had lost. They were just careless.

It is only in looking back that I detach a narrative about my parents from
all the rest. I didn't know much about them, though down on the floor of
the ocean, where I lived in my child world, I could sense disturbances up
above on the surface of the water. We used to rock for hours at night:
two children to a bed, one at the bottom, one at the top, arms crossed,
rocking and rocking. Nor was I living just in this world. I had another
world. In school, I ruined the nun's Christmas tableau. I was the
Archangel Gabriel, and I had to stand behind Joseph and Mary and the
Infant Jesus on a kitchen chair and look down on them piously and hold
my arms strapped to great feather contraptions—my wings—over
them. But I saw someone I knew in the audience, and I waved my wing
at her. The nun was so angry afterwards that she broke the chair to hit
me with a leg of it. Yet I walked home leaving room between me and the
verge of the road, as always, for my Guardian Angel.

Then we went for a while to a different primary school. My mother
sometimes didn't get up in the mornings and we had to go out empty-
handed, though she would come down later on the bike she had learned

to ride and pass a pudding bowl of potatoes in salad cream through the bars of the playground. But when we had lunches we put them with everyone else's in a cupboard in the room. Sometimes we'd hear a chomping noise. "Miss! Miss! The rat is in the cupboard!" The teacher would swing the door open and hit the rat with the shovel she had for the stove. On the way home from that school, for a long time, I climbed down into a quarry where a pool of water had collected, and there was a rusted barrel on its side in the water. If I lay down and looked along the surface of the water in the barrel at eye-level, I would see lovely little fairies, with straight partings in their blond hair and pink ballet skirts. They were about the size of flies.

I knew other places besides home. They sent me to Kerry, to the relations. There were pig hairs in the yellowy skin of the fatty boiled bacon the lady draped across the cabbage I had to eat. But on Saturday nights a technicolour pudding was installed in the parlour, under a white cloth; we got that after Sunday Mass. The north Dublin fields where we lived were silent and bleak, so it was like going to New York to be sent to my great-aunt in Athlone. She was the mistress of a tiny, hardly used pub, Egan's of Connaught Street. Mr. Egan kept a big hoinking pig in the slimy yard. Myself and Auntie Kit used to go around the public grass of the Battery on our hands and knees, collecting a certain weed for the bristly old thing with its watery eyes. The shed the pig slept in was full of disintegrating sheet music from when Kit as a young woman had been a pianist accompanying the silent movies in Listowel. "Me and Jane in a plane/Soaring up in the sky;/No traffic cop/Will ever stop/Me and Jane in a plane." I loved the streets of Athlone: the lights, the chip shop, Broderick's Bakery a few doors away where a machine sliced the pans. I was even a small celebrity among the street's boys and girls, being thought to be from Dublin city.

There was the big world, too, presenting us isolated children with puzzles. I went into a shop one day. The woman behind the counter was showing something—big photos—in a low-voiced, secret way to another women, bent over the counter. I glimpsed the photos. They were of desperate bony fingers reaching out from under the wooden walls of huts. Fingers like sticks. These were photos from the Holocaust. I saw gas ovens. Piles of bones. That night our friends came across the field, for us to go down the railway line and rob Williams's orchard as usual. But as we were going along I told them about the evil in the world, and we all decided to repent. We went home and upended the kitchen chairs to kneel at and said a very long Rosary. A year later—we were now living in a temporary cottage—the maid, who was never paid and never went out, fell to the floor and gave birth to a baby. It transpired that the butcher, when he called with the meat, had been having sex with her. The baby went to the maid's mother. My mother happened to call on that house a few weeks later. The baby was emaciated, immobile, sinking into death. "Sure, who wants it?" the grandmother said. It did die, as far as I know. It was 1953. Then we were again in a new school. We were assembled in the concert hall to listen to the Coronation of Queen Elizabeth in Westminster Abbey on the convent radio. "Always remember, girls," the nun said, "that 'God Save the Queen' is the most noble tune ever penned in eight bars."

I started looking at things. We used to come in from the country to visit my nana, my father's mother. I don't know how it was allowed, but when we got to her house, a bit down Clonliffe Road from my mother's family house, I would go out again and start walking. I could not get enough of looking at Dublin, which was Joyce's Dublin still, then, brown and dusty and dense with street life.

Later in life, my father told me things about the city. He told me that the sea used to come in at the North Strand, which is why it is called a strand, and that they reclaimed Fairview Park with the rubble from the ruins of O'Connell Street after the Rising. They laid a rail and a trolley to transport the rubble out, and the bright young people after a night out would jump on the bogey-car in their gowns and tails and push it off and come whizzing out from town. But when I walked around Dublin as a child I knew nothing, except what I noted with my own eyes, like a spy behind enemy lines. I would walk along Summerhill, which was a canyon of Georgian tenements then, with women sitting on the worn and beautiful front steps all the day long. I'd read the writing on statues. I liked NE PLUS ULTRA on the Parnell one, though I did not know what it meant. I would go into the Protestant cathedrals and go down the quays, and around behind the distillery in Smithfield, and stop to look at anything: a horse and cart backing into a yard, a woman calling down from a window, a butcher emptying a basin of pink water into the gutter. No one sees a child watching. I was never afraid till I went to *The Messiah* in the Theatre Royal when I was eleven, and a man put his hand up under my skirt and hurt me with his fingers.

Perhaps that habit of observation helped me to get my job with *The Irish Times*. I was offered a try at writing a column, as far as I know, because of a conversation I had, in the late 1980s, about the physical beauty of the seaside places north of Dublin when I was a child. I had this conversation with Gay Byrne, on his *Gay Byrne Radio Show*. I was a television producer with RTÉ then—Radio Telifís Éireann—and I'd read somewhere that if you watched a year's television only three percent of the human faces you would see would be those of women over, say, fifty or fifty-five; older women only figure on television in ads and soap operas. So I had made a series of short programmes in which elderly Irishwomen just looked into the camera and told the story of their lives. The women's personalities, and the twists and turns of their lives, and the compelling effect of a face looking out at the viewer without any intervening interviewer had added up to something strong. The series won a Jacob's Award, which had been presented the night before, and Gay was interviewing me on his programme as a result.

Gay Byrne reminds me of my father—whom he knew, of course. My father and Eamonn Andrews were doing a kind of "In Town Tonight" programme on Radio Éireann when Gay was starting out in broadcasting, too. The careers of the three men could have gone any way; that they ended where each of them did was due as much to chance as to their talents. The three of them shared a kind of impersonal charm—an ability to stand in a room and be the one others wanted to please, rather than the one to work at pleasing. They each found ways of keeping their dignity against the flattery of a small town.

Gay evokes for me—not that he means to—my father's mild and decorous childhood home in Clonliffe Road, where no one ever used the front door, dressed in its striped canvas blind, and down in the basement my grandmother swept the bobbled chenille tablecloth with its own little brush and pan after the meals—rabbit stews, rice puddings—she served to my granda and my auntie when they came home from their respectable jobs at dinner hour. Gay's people and my father's people would have been alike, I think. Mass for the women every morning, and First Fridays, Novenas, the seven churches on Holy Thursday, Tenebrae on Good Friday, Exposition of the Sacred Sacrament, and so on. At Christmas, card games and the odd bottle of stout and the married sons and the handful of old friends calling. No new kind of people ever coming into the house. No new opinions or ways of behaving penetrating it. The only fiction, the didactic fable at the back of each copy of the *Messenger of the Sacred Heart*. Even history was somewhat frowned upon for showing off. I pressed my grandmother about the Rising. "Oh, yes, there was terrible trouble in town that year," she said, her face wrinkling up with disapproval. "We could hear it all from here." Then she brightened. "But we got vegetables in 1916 that we never got before or since! The carts from Rush couldn't get into the city with all the trouble. They could only get as far as Drumcondra—here, at the top of Clonliffe Road—and we'd go up and get the best of vegetables for half nothing!"

Gay and my father both transcended the cautiousness of their backgrounds, though Gay was more committed than my father to the values of that background. If the two of them walked towards me now, I'd see two dapper, smallish men with attractive voices and quick minds, both using a natural charm and courtesy to keep other people at a distance from them. Behind Gay I'd see an orderly and consistent life. Behind my father, chaos accumulated.

But around 1950, in the place Gay and I were talking about that day on the radio—in the pristine countryside to the north of Dublin with its string of seaside villages—my father and my family were still well. He responded to even that quiet countryside with brisk enjoyment. He took us on walks through the woods and told us what "Indian file" meant. He planted potatoes and named the ridges after the stations on the Dublin–Belfast railway line.

Where we lived was beautiful, then. Not the big flat fields around the bungalow—though even there, on a winter afternoon, I saw my first heron rise into the sky from a pond, grey on grey—but the beaches and the cornfields and the old woods. And the winding country roads, so little used then—at Malahide and Rob's Walls and the front at Portmarnock—that sand drifted across them and collected on them. In winter great wild waves crashed up the sand at Portmarnock and broke over the road, and across from the dunes there was a little wooden pub and some holiday shacks and then fields. The road around the estuary to Baldoyle flooded quickly and silently in winter, and we ran along the grassy bank to school between silver sheets of floodwater. There were no new houses. The parkland and fine houses of the landlords stretched back almost to the edge of the city. Near us, there was a deserted big house, shuttered and silent in the middle of woods. The peacocks had been left behind there and gone wild, and they called to each other all the night. We walked a mile to where the bus from Dublin turned around. It was a country bus, going through countryside on its way into town, stopping at the pubs that marked each little hamlet. Everything was clean and bright.

At the shabby end of the main street of Malahide, where the air was scented by a little candy factory, you turned down past a decrepit, elegant terrace, and at the bottom, at the water's edge, a man with a rowboat would take you across to the sand and marram grass of Malahide Island, where seabirds' eggs lay lavishly on the ground, as at the Creation. You rang a big bell on a pole at the end of the day, and the boatman came back across the water, shining and still in the evening, to collect you. Or you stayed on Malahide beach with your jam sandwiches and bottle of milk, and the people in the houses would boil your kettle for the tea for a penny.

That sparkling world was what I was talking to Gay Byrne about, on the radio that day. He has an intimate appreciation of how idyllic north Dublin once was and what we have lost. But I remember trying to convince him that Ireland is a much, much better place now than it used to be, even though so much beauty has disappeared with development. When the interview was over, I went back to the day's ordinary work. But Conor Brady, then deputy editor of *The Irish Times*, rang me. I'd never met him, but I knew who he was. He'd heard me on the car radio. Would I like to try my hand at a few opinion columns? This was the circumstance that led to this last, deeply satisfying decade of my life— and to this book, of course. Conspiracy theorists, who think that columnists are carefully chosen for their "liberal" views, had better apply to Conor Brady to identify the conspiracy. He never said what he heard in me that made him ring me. I wasn't talking about my views. I was talking, to someone who reminded me of my dead father, about a long-ago childhood.

2

The most useful thing I brought out of my childhood was confidence in reading. Not long ago, I went on a weekend self-exploratory workshop, in the hope of getting a clue about how to live. One of the exercises we were given was to make a list of the ten most important events of our lives—the key moments that brought us from birth to wherever we are now. Number one was: "I was born," and you could put whatever you liked after that. Without even thinking about it my hand wrote, at number two: "I learnt to read." "I was born and I learnt to read" wouldn't be a sequence that occurs to many people, I imagine. But I knew what I meant to say. Being born was something done to me, but my own life began—I began for myself—when I first made out the meaning of a sentence.

I remember everything about it. The page was a double-column, small-type account of someone's verbatim evidence in a Scottish murder trial. I don't know how it made its way to north County Dublin. But I was puzzling at a line when all of a sudden the meaning of one word I understood hopped across—like the Ping-Pong ball hopping along the line in a sing-along—to join the meaning of the next word I understood, until there were enough words that meant something to make sense of the sentence. I was overcome with delight. I was still small—not yet four. But I ran across the field and up the road, speeding along through the summer dust—I see it as if it were yesterday—to the shop, a long distance away. "I can read! I can read!" I shouted up at the woman who ran the shop. She bent down. "Well, aren't you the great little girl!"

I must have picked it up already from my mother—that reading is a defence. That "they" can't get at you when you have a book. Of course my mother was the "they" in this case. Any demand she made—get sticks to start the fire, take the baby for a walk in the pram—interfered with my reading. I found ease and comfort in books. The little Carnegie Library in the village, complete with display cases of dusty exhibits like an ivory back scratcher from an Egyptian tomb, was a cornucopia, even though the pitch-pine bookshelves were half empty. I don't remember a children's section. I read all the volumes of James Agate's diaries, though I hardly knew what a London theatre critic was. I read all the volumes of *Stories from the Opera*. The library didn't get new books very often. A teacher lent me *Anne of Green Gables* and *The Road to Avonlea*; I nearly died of pleasure. In Newcomen Mall library I got *Heidi*. I read the easy bits of *Ulysses*. I made no distinction between children's literature and other literature. For a while the Americans had a library in Dublin; it was part of the United States Information Service. My mother borrowed books there, and I read them after her: Dos Passos, Dreiser. And there were a few books at home. André Maurois's life of Shelley. A thriller by Francis Stuart with the pages of the dénouement missing. *Bright Day* by J. B. Priestley. Its epigraph was the first line from Shakespeare I ever encountered.

I liked the words as much as the plots. In a scandalous book called *The Kansas City Milkman*—Mammy vaguely said I shouldn't read it—one character said about a woman, "What she needs is a roll in the hay." I didn't know what this meant—I saw a barn, in my head—but I loved its being a metaphor. A local boy was known as Buggy. "Don't call me that," he said. "I've a handle to me mug the same as you have." I murmured it over to myself: "A handle to me mug. . . ." Halfway up the hill in Malahide there was a bench, with a little plaque on it that said PRO

BONO PUBLICO. And on the side of the Chef sauce bottle—often on the table—there was a vertical column of words. Piquant was one of them. "Piquant," I would say to myself as I dodged along beside the gurgling ditches on my way to school. "Piquant. Appetising." Best of all was the beginning of the Last Gospel—in those days, it was said at the end of every Mass: "In the beginning was the word and the word was with God and the word was God. . . ." I loved the sonority of it, and that it was meaningful although I didn't know what it meant. No one was ashamed of words, at home. The teacher took us into a room in one school to listen to Daddy doing a commentary in Irish as well as English from an army Tattoo on the radio.

But really respectable people were cautious in speech. The girls at school would say to me sourly, if I used an unusual word, "Did you swallow a dictionary, or what?" They had more sense than to risk exposing their selves in essays that might be read out. My essays were always being read out. There I'd be, a confused and emotional exhibitionist, and there they'd be, silent and politic. Being known to be imaginative made you marginal because it was close to "making a show of yourself," drawing attention, showing off, exaggerating, telling lies. I was more an entertainer than a serious student because it was a useless thing like English I was good at. Girls were good at English, not boys. Because of all this, the women who taught English had an intense secret life. They slipped books to fellow enthusiasts, like Russians passing samizdat literature along the underground. I went to seven schools. I was no good at anything else, but I was good at English. I needed the love I got from English teachers, and I returned it, and return it.

"I don't know whether she's intelligent, Sister," my father said, when he delivered me to the Mother Superior of my last school, "but she and her mother can take a book apart." I see him saying this, sitting in the shiny brown parlour, automatically trying to charm the nun as quickly as possible. He was paying me a compliment, certainly, but one he could place at a genially baffled distance from his own powers. Since I knew, too, that Mammy was his dependant, not he hers, it wasn't such a great thing to be lumped in with her.

It was at secondary school that reading books took on depth and became the study of English. From then on, all my life and still today, reading for pleasure and reading for study or work were never very different from each other. After school—to digress—I did formally study English at University College Dublin, and after UCD I worked on medieval English prose romances at the University of Hull, and eventually, back in Dublin, I prepared for an examination on the whole course of English literature for a big scholarship, and when I got that I did a B.Phil. in English at Oxford. And I suppose I've read a book every few days throughout my life. Apart from a few writers who don't make up in anything else for their lack of inner life—Chaucer, a lot of Balzac, Scott, the jollier Dickens, Salman Rushdie—and apart from a few writers I'm completely cut off from—Lamartine, Hawthorne, Richardson—I have enjoyed everything of any importance I've ever read. In any case, I would prefer to read something I don't enjoy than do almost anything else. I like the act of reading in itself. Following the line of something—not just the story but the rhythm, the tone, the feel of what has accumulated from before and what is beginning to impend—becoming surefooted on the high-wire of the author's intention. I liked everything to do with English as a school subject. Textbooks. Vocabularies—the set anthologies of my day began with examples of metrical schemes and figures of speech, words to marvel at, like rodomontade, anapaest, or onomatopoeia. I liked English exams—I remember drawing a diagram of the shape Shelley's "Ode to the West Wind" made inside my head as a treat for the examiner, on the blotting-paper sheet, at the exam we did halfway through secondary school.

Reading certain books was a complex and complete experience. I had a room in a squalid mews in Dublin for a while when I was a student; the landlord had whips hanging from his bedstead. I remember it only because one summer morning I settled in the weedy yard when I had done the housework and began reading *Madame Bovary*. Hours later, the sun had moved to the other wall, and my heart was beating heavily as Flaubert led me, under his perfect control, into the last chapter. I remember gasping—involuntary light gasps—as Henry James added another circle to the rings of consequence that expanded from the actions of the principals in *The Wings of the Dove*, until the void settles around Densher and Kate. I lived in a hotel in Teheran for a few months in the 1970s. The revolution was near. Men with machine-guns patrolled the lobby in front of the elevators. Places you could buy alcohol—dim shops like cupboards in the alleyways around the Russian embassy—were closing down. I didn't care. Every evening I'd hurry back to my room to pour out a glass of mild Iranian vodka and settle with perfect happiness into wherever I'd got to in *Remembrance of Things Past*. It took me eleven weeks to read Proust, that first time. His world was my real world; I just bore with the days, exotic as they were, until I could get back to it.

And Yeats. At various times in my life, themes or tones of Yeats have been the only right ones. These days, the grave and majestic turn at the end of "Meditation in Time of Civil War," where he pays his respects to Wordsworth and to reality and acknowledges his own incompleteness, is especially meaningful to me:

> But O! ambitious heart, had such a proof drawn forth
> A company of friends, a conscience set at ease,
> It had but made us pine the more. The abstract joy,
> The half-read wisdom of daemonic images,
> Suffice the ageing man as once the growing boy.

The simplicity of the last line—arrived at, after all the complexities of the poem—moves me almost to tears. This passage, and all the other bits and pieces which are in my memory, are always available. There is grandeur in there, no matter what appears to be happening: waiting at traffic lights, peeling potatoes. I learnt T. S. Eliot's "Portrait of a Lady" when I was fourteen or fifteen and an enthusiast of world-weariness. My head would be full of the smell of hyacinths across a garden, conjuring up things that other people—Eliot and myself being too fastidious—had desired. To look at, I was just a spotty girl.

If there were nothing else, reading would—obviously—be worth living for. Saul Bellow. Alice Munro. Chekhov. Keats. Eoin MacNamee. Montherlant. James. James Joyce. Tolstoy. Mailer. Dacia Maraini. Dermot Healy. Douglas Dunn. Trollope. Richard Ford. *Caoineadh Airt Uí Laoghaire*. Donne. Colette. Robert Lowell. *Jane Eyre*. Naipaul. Kafka's "Up in the Gallery." Roddy Doyle. John McGahern. Racine. Kawabata. I don't have to observe any hierarchy. But I recognise that there is a hierarchy. There is great and less great and so on, down to trash.

When I was a teacher I had to avoid quoting some things because they moved me so deeply I was afraid I'd cry in front of the students. The big speeches in *King Lear* did that, and the end of *The Tempest*. And "Death be not proud," and "So we'll go no more a-roving." And what Ralph says to Isabel Archer just before he dies, in *Portrait of a Lady*. And Keats's wonderful letters. I presented writing like this to my students with confidence, just as it had been confidently presented to me. I think classic literature is deservedly so-called. I might never have read *Phèdre* or "Dejection: An Ode" or *Samson Agonistes* or *Les Liaisons Dangereuses* or Pope or Hopkins or Ben Jonson but that they were prescribed "texts." I don't have any objection to the art made by dead white males. Far from it: The thought that I might have missed this literature—that I might have been born later, when it was decided it was too difficult for young people—fills me with horror. I never think of gender when I'm reading. If questions about it force themselves on me, I have to come out of reading, into this world.

And I like what derives from literature—fine commentary, like Cynthia Ozick's or Seamus Heaney's or Henry James's prefaces. Biography. Autobiography. The only thing I don't read much of now, when time is so precious, are middle-range authors—Kundera, say, or Paul Auster. Writers who play middle-level games. When I want pleasure I want perfect trivia—romances by Judith Krantz, thrillers by Scott

Turow, moral tales by Maeve Binchy. Or else I want the real, the great thing.

The worst deprivation of boarding-school was that we weren't allowed to have fiction in our possession. I longed for it as someone thirsty longs for water, because the language of the school was Irish, and I couldn't read Irish and could barely speak it. I was half gagged all the time. On a few very special feast days the "library"—a glass-fronted bookcase—was opened. You had an afternoon to devour as much as you could of, say, Annie P. Smithson. But every year some young Frenchwoman would come to the convent, to help with teaching French, and though she slept in a cubicle in the dormitory like us, the usual rules did not apply to her, and she often had novels in her locker. I needed them so badly that I made the stories out through the barrier of French: *Les Clés du Royaume* and all the rest of A. J. Cronin; *La Chatelaine du Liban*. Novels were about what I cared about. They asked the questions I wanted answered. How do lives get lived? How is love found?

3

I was sent to boarding-school—where I arrived on my fourteenth birthday—because puberty got me into so much trouble. Not that I knew what it was called or what was happening; all I knew was that something had run over me like a train and simplified everything. I was stunned by the demands of the body I had barely noticed before. I didn't care for anybody or anything in the small town we lived in except going to dances and being walked home, or wandering around the dark and windy lanes that led down to the harbour in the town, talking to my friend about boys. My father came upon us mooching furtively along. "Button your coat!" he snapped at me. "You look like a mill girl."

It wasn't just my sexuality he was recoiling from; I was becoming déclassé. In that town then, the convent girls didn't go to the Town Hall to jostle at the mirror in the Jeyes Fluid–smelling Ladies and then sit on the bench at the edge of the dance floor, burningly aware of the males around, waiting to be asked up to dance, till four in the morning. Only working people, or people who went to the Tech, danced. By the time the band had got to "Good night, sweetheart, / See you in the morning," the hall was a sweaty, shuffling mass of solid eroticism. After the national anthem and finding my coat, I'd go out into the dark night.

Whoever was "leaving me home" would be waiting in the shadows past the streetlamp, speechless. Often, we didn't know each other's name.

For the sake of those bouts of devouring each other—in doorways, against trees, under the wall of our house—I would do anything. For instance, I stole. My mother was poorer than ever. She made me do a humiliating thing every so often—go to the gasworks, down behind the harbour, and walk past the men to the office, and ask for a man to call to the house to free our jammed gas meter. Everyone knew the meter wasn't jammed, but when he counted the money there might be a few shillings surplus and she was desperate for them. Still, I took her money to pay into the dances.

The nuns knew everything about the town. When they heard I was being left home by a married man—I didn't know that or anything else except that I was wild about him—they called in my father to tell him to take me away from the school. I was thirteen. I was supposed to be bad.

I was the second eldest. My parents still had the energy to do something about my crisis. My mother, on the telephone from the Red Bank bar, got me into St. Louis's Convent, far away in Monaghan. My father sold his car. I was bought a trousseau in Gorevan's: napkin rings, three pairs of shoes, a dressing gown, a hairbrush—things no one in the family had ever had before. Then he borrowed another car—putting himself out for me to an extent that I still feel guilty about, compared to the care my brothers and sisters got—and drove me to Monaghan himself. There was snow on the roads, and he couldn't manage the strange gears, and it took us two days to get there. But in the end, on an Ash Wednesday in midterm, we went to Mass together, and then he brought me up to the grey granite building and left me with the Mother Superior. There were shards of ice on the lake in front of the school and motionless swans on the black water. Not much more than a week before I had been slow-waltzing half the night, pressed into men's bodies by their big heavy hands on my back. By comparison, I had now landed on a planet that could not support life.

. . .

I had to forget, when I was away at school, what I knew about bodies. Yet when I was at home in the holidays, I was in the company of girls whose destiny was marriage, not further education. Their lives depended on the quality of the man they got, and the only way to get a man was to go courting. So the important things in life—the career tools— were manner, figure, clothes, carefully judged liberties allowed to this boyfriend or that. By the mid-1950s my family had moved to a house in Dublin, in Clontarf. My sister and her friends were soon working in offices and shops and could buy some clothes and makeup for themselves. When I came home, I didn't belong. I'd go to hops and not get asked up at all. I was dowdy. I didn't know the argot. *Rock Around the Clock* came to Dublin, and cinema seats were ripped up. The idea that young people are different from older people in every way was starting, with Elvis and James Dean. But up on the border in our Irish-speaking convent we were simply imperfect adults, living somewhere between twenty and two hundred years in the past. I was sent back there after every holidays—pale from smoking, hollow-eyed from silent explorations with boys in bus shelters—no matter how hard I argued that I would be better off getting a job in Clery's department store. "I could hand up money," I'd say. No one listened. When I got to school there was no one I could talk to about what I'd done in the holidays, any more than when I went home there was anyone interested in what happened at school.

But school had its own tangy, dense atmosphere. It was a complicated, cerebral place. We might as well have been disembodied spirits for all the attention that was paid to our bodies. Getting out of bed in the dark mornings was hard, and we got chilblains and pimples, and we weren't allowed to wash our hair often enough or take enough baths. If there were others like myself who already knew something about sensuality, I presume they suppressed the knowledge, as I did. (It was to be another twenty years before, idle on a bed in Paris on a hot afternoon, masturbation re-emerged from where it had hidden since kindergarten.)

Our underwear was inspected. Stockings fell in wrinkles from grey elastic garters. Girls outside wore high conical bras those days, but our young breasts were flattened by our gym slips, and you could see nipples through the fabric. There was a laywoman who came in to school to teach. She had what might have been two puppies wriggling in her jumper just above her waistband. We never mentioned such things.

Any luxury was most intensely felt. The classes who didn't have a state exam did an operetta at Christmas. To the exam-doers, coming from an evening of silent study, scurrying past the *halla cheoil* to late prayers in the dim, cold chapel, the sound of the soaring orchestra and chorus as they reached the finale inside—"We do not heed their di-is-ma-al sound," the year they did *The Mikado*—was beautiful. It coloured the wintry night. On the morning of St. Patrick's Day, too, girls from the orchestra sat out on chairs with their fiddles and played a jaunty jig as we hurried past to a special Mass. There were daffodils in a vase in the refectory, and a fat little sausage each, to mark the feast day. Anything special—an extra half-hour's sleep, a parcel from home, a puff of another girl's talcum powder, the little altars we made to Our Lady in our cubicles in the month of May, a fresh loaf when we expected stale, two pats of butter instead of one—was deeply pleasurable.

School was full of tingling excitement, too. When I mentioned this recently, to the only nun I still know, she said angrily, "Oh, no, Nuala! For heaven's sake don't be coming out with all that!" But there is nothing to be ashamed of in how we made a romantic system to contain our rampant emotions. There were boarding-schools all over Ireland then, and all of them must have had girls who had crushes on other girls and on nuns. And each place must have had a special vocabulary peculiar to that sub-world, all those words and concepts that will be lost forever when women my age die, because no one values them enough to record them. In Monaghan, the girl with the crush was called a "daftie"; a popular senior girl might have eight or ten dafties. The dafties competed to get the loved one to accept presents. The point of the present was to be thanked for it. You hung around, perhaps for weeks, always knowing exactly where in any crowd the loved one was located and whether she was moving towards you or away from you, for the saliva-drying excitement of the moment when she might mutter a few words of thanks. Being thanked was called a "soirée"—pronounced swarry by us. (Perhaps the term survived from the nineteenth century, when the St. Louis sisters came from France to Ireland.) After a soirée, your friends would have to help you walk, your legs would be so wobbly. The few nuns who played this delicious game had great scope for effect; they might thank you among the dim rosebushes in the nuns' graveyard.

The emotions we felt as schoolgirls were volatile and exaggerated, and they have always been despised by the world. But they were not trivial. They were a grounding in the affective dimension that was to matter most to us all our lives. They were not a mere substitute for what we would have been doing with boys if we weren't in boarding-school, which is what the patriarchy has always arrogantly presumed. Emotion was an element in the process of our putting ourselves together—learning appropriateness, learning control, learning to differentiate our selves from the other selves around. The satisfaction of feelings was the engine that drove us on, rather than competitiveness or ambition. There was a nun who was tempestuous and brilliant, who strode everywhere, a high colour on her handsome face. Engagement with her on the level of feelings was serious and fine, finer by far than any relationship I had known before. She bent our incoherent feelings to the purposes of learning and talking and thinking—to goals beyond personal gratification. At the time I was ashamed of my own emotionalism. I admired the girls and nuns who held themselves apart. Not long ago, I stopped the car in a remote part of Ireland where I was lost, to ask a woman walking along ahead of me the way. She turned out to have been at Monaghan at the same time I was. She remembered me, but I, to my embarrassment, did not remember her. "Oh, I wouldn't expect you to," she said. "I wasn't the kind of girl Sister was interested in. You were." That was a compliment, but a bitter one.

Not everyone can have forgotten all this. A girl I was the daftie of back then contacted me not long ago to see whether I could help her residents' association to save their local church from demolition. I could hardly say to this respectable matron, "Do you remember the afternoon I lay on the outside of the counterpane when you were ill in bed, and I told you the fine hairs at your hairline were the most beautiful things I'd ever seen?" And near me there's a pub where a group of rather smart workmates—perhaps they're estate agents—sometimes have a drink after work. One of them waves to me. I remember the pretty necklace she gave me when she was my daftie. It says something about the way the sexuality of girls, and even their innocent sublimation of sexuality, is stigmatised, that if I were to indicate to her that I remember, she would faint with shame.

I'm not ashamed of our fervours. But I am ashamed that twice I stole the gifts I gave to my heroine. I took Tweed talc or round soaps in tissue paper from other girls' cubicles. I had to. I had no money. I didn't take them for myself, just to give to her. I think that she may have known—and that the nuns knew and never came out with it. They knew I told lies. They knew I read under the blanket. They knew (this was nearly the end of me) that I smoked, perched in the window embrasure of a lavatory high up in the attics, listening at the cold glass to the noises of the town, like the great roars from the rallies for the IRA men—one of them was a local—who were killed on the Border in 1956. They knew that it got harder and harder to get my fees from my parents (though as it was I was costing the family a fortune, with my uniform and my books). My mother sometimes got a crony from the pub she drank in to drive her up to Monaghan, but she was afraid of the nuns, so she would stay in the bar of the hotel in town and send the crony to get me out of the convent. The nuns probably knew about my thefts. I think they were probably enormously kind. But they weren't straight with me. I didn't trust them, any more than they trusted me.

I have no doubt that being sent to this school was the biggest single stroke of luck in my life. When I have criticised it in the past, the nun I'm friendly with has gently suggested that I brought a troubled self to the school—that I projected my own unhappinesses onto it. It does frighten me that I remember the bad times rather than the good ones. "But don't you remember when you led the strike?" she says. "Don't you remember the special Virgil grinds and how exciting they were? Don't you remember the fun we had rehearsing *Blossom Time*? Your essay that we published in *The Oriflamme*? The time I lent you 'J. Alfred Prufrock'?" I'm middle-aged now. I don't want to be engrossed in old hurts. But they are there. The time the nuns ostracised me because I didn't go straight to the chapel to thank God for coming first in Ireland in French. ("No, Nuala, it was certainly not a punishment. It was just that we're very, very disappointed in you.") The time they wouldn't let me be a Child of Mary. The time my friend Breda and I had to apologise on our knees in front of the whole school for taking bread from the refectory, because we were hungry.

We were expected to be the best in Ireland at school subjects. But also to be more than exam-passers—to appreciate art, for instance, though, music apart, "art" might be an illuminated scroll, recording the prayers that had gone into a spiritual bouquet, or a recitation, with gestures, of "Glory to God but there it is/The dawn on the hills of Ireland" for a visiting American bishop. We did debates. There were engravings after Claude and Poussin on the walls. But intelligence or artistry were nothing much in themselves. They were to be put at the service of God. The nuns were the most powerful women in Ireland. But they didn't have any ideals for the secular world. The thing that would bring a girl most praise was a desire to enter the convent, to be a Bride of Christ. When I left school, the head nun—who could have run General Motors, she was so competent—advised me, earnestly, that in whatever situation I might find myself I should think what the Virgin Mary would have done and do the same.

I left school, full of furtive resentments against it, and didn't go back for thirty years. But there's a small museum open to the public in a yard of the buildings now. One day, driving through Monaghan, I thought I might sneak in and maybe get a look at the hidden courtyard and the glassed-in corridor—scenes of such epic events in my adolescence—without meeting anyone. But as I hurried into the museum, a nun came flying down a fire escape. "Nuala! Nuala!" she cried, with unmistakable delight in her voice. I couldn't believe it—someone here remembered me by name after so long! This particular nun I recalled with untroubled affection. She had taught languages with clear-minded vigour. But when she linked my arm and took me—protesting—to meet the terrible ogre who had been the head nun in my time, I was even more amazed. "We're so proud of all you've done, Nuala, and it's wonderful to see you looking so well. You'd be—let's see—you'll be forty-seven soon now, won't you?" This person, in all the world, remembered my birthday! They wove a little feeling of family around the tea they gave me in the nun's parlour. Afterwards, I helped Mother Dorothea—tiny and frail—to shuffle into the chapel, where she said a prayer and I stood transfixed. Then she kissed me, and I ran out and got into the car and bent over the steering wheel, crying too hard to drive.

When I got going, a mile or so down the road, I saw a phone box. I rang my friend Marian who'd been at the same school ten years after me, and who knew the dread Mother Dorothea had evoked in generations of girls. "We were wrong, Marian," I sobbed down the phone at her. "They really liked us. They understood the girls: they just didn't let it show!"

"Our first revisionist," Marian said.

4

I left school after the Leaving Cert, when I was seventeen. I hoped to go to college, but it would be awhile before I could do the entrance scholarship exam and another while until I would know whether I'd won a scholarship. I also hoped I wouldn't get into college so I could get a job as an assistant in Clery's, like my friend. At that time, young men as well as young women worked behind the counters in the old wooden-floored Clery's, where the cash zinged around the shop on pulleys and burst up from vacuum pipes. The shop assistants seemed to me to have the best of fun. I had a job, but I had no company in it, working as a clerk in the hire-purchase office of a furniture shop in Grafton Street. Hire-purchase was for the very poor, then. The customers walked down a long room to the hatch where I sat. I saw from the way they walked towards me how bitter it was for them to be still paying out for things they'd got long ago. Money was dominating me, too. I was living at home but I was giving up half my wages to Mammy. From leaving school on, how to earn enough money to keep myself was my biggest single problem for years and years.

In that interval between school and college, I was as devout as I was ever going to be. I joined the Legion of Mary in Dublin; we had a hand-cart displaying pious literature near O'Connell Street, and we had a special mission to streetwalkers. I said prayers every day, and I went to Mass. I did read during the tedious bits of Mass, a ploy discovered in Monaghan where we were sometimes marched through the town—longingly past the sweetshops and the fish-and-chip shop—and up the hill to the cathedral, across from its twin hill where hunched figures prowled the paths of the lunatic asylum. I read, concealed in my missal, anything that was a bit religious—the poems and sermons of John Donne, for instance. I was a member of the Pioneer Total Abstinence Association; when I did take my first drink I went back to it, and then again, and again. . . . I went to Confession a lot, to help me with boys.

One of the reasons I was doing my best to be a normal girl and a good Catholic was the terrible shock of losing my virginity. A while earlier, home on holidays from school, I'd been messing with a boyfriend on a sofa in his house. His mother was upstairs. Lionel Hampton was on the record player, plinking out "So High the Moon." My panties were off. The boy suddenly, terrifyingly, pushed into me, all the way. I ran along the suburban streets to home, panting, crying, praying out loud not to get pregnant. I locked myself in the bathroom to wash off the blood and kneel, in privacy, to beg Our Lady to save me. Some of the girls I hung around with had come up the stairs to the bathroom door and were taunting me through it; I must have said something, when I ran the gauntlet of them, sitting on the wall outside. "What happened to your knickers?" they shouted, like the Furies. "What happened to your knickers?" The fear and revulsion drove me almost into believing that I had a vocation to be a nun. But the more lasting effect was that I was enthusiastic with boys from about the waist up, but the rest of me was so self-conscious that I wouldn't even say that I wanted to go to the Ladies.

When I knew that I'd got the scholarship to UCD I went on holidays to my aunt, who had been such fun when I was a child. She was living in someone else's house in a dreary east-coast seaside resort where the sea went out so far at low tide that you couldn't see it. We sat at night under the seawall in our coats, and she drank whiskey from the half-pint bottle of whiskey she always had, by now, in her handbag. She was like a loving child, herself. But she had become baffled. She knew she loved her own children, and us, her sister's children. But she didn't know why she was married at all or why to the particular man who was her husband or why she was afraid of Grandad or why anything. She was always called "wild." Her husband worked abroad. She was summoned off to live with him from time to time. More than once, she drank the ticket money, so as to get out of going. But then her husband and her father would arrange her deportation over her head.

My family's house in Clontarf was packed and clamorous. My father was "Terry O'Sullivan" through and through now; the idealistic schoolteacher and lieutenant in the Army, Tomás O'Faolain, who had called his wife his *chroidhe dhil*—beloved heart—when he wrote with such affection and energy about the arrangements for the moving of their little family to Donegal, had been overtaken by another identity. Partly it was the size the family grew to, along with my mother's refusal to be satisfied with serving it, that killed his enthusiasm. But mostly he was alienated from a domestic role by the opportunity which the modernising of Ireland happened to present to him. He was not a journalist in the ordinary meaning of the word. He was a small god, in the world—which was then very new and innocent—of people who wanted publicity.

His successor on the newspaper gossip column "Dubliner's Diary," the distinguished journalist Michael O'Toole, talks in a reminiscence he published about the way my father made semi-majestic entrances into this or that event around town. Holding himself aloof, he would wait, with melancholy calm, for the customary adulation. He would have risen in our house out on the seafront in Clontarf around two in the afternoon, and freshly washed and shaved, and often wearing evening clothes, he would have stepped into the car from the newspaper, when the driver brought it to the gate, to read his invitations under the special reading light that had been installed over the back seat. He would make a round of social events until settling down in his office to write, around midnight, a "Dubliner's Diary" for the next day's *Evening Press*. Restaurateurs would send exotic meals under silver cloches, and wines and brandy, to the office. He banged out the "Diary" on his old typewriter come what may, with the discipline that was his second nature.

He wouldn't have spent more than a couple of hours, awake, in his home. When he was a young father, an old woman who worked for my parents told me recently, he always spoke Irish to Grainne and me, the two eldest. Now he had no time to speak much to his children in any language. When he was a young husband—this woman told me unwittingly—he and my mother were very close. "I think they must have fought a lot," she said to me. "When he came home from work he used to tell me to take you children out for a walk and not come back for an hour." Nobody knows the interior of other people's marriages, and the one and only thing my mother was confident about all her life was the perfection of their physical relationship. But he avoided home. Even on Christmas Day, when we had charming rituals to do with the tree and presents and champagne—things we'd always done, like a family in a book—he eventually went out. He often took a child or children or his wife to a function, or arranged a treat for them from some grateful hotelier or the like. But he never spent a full day at home. And my mother wasn't at home much, either. She went up to the pub two times in the day. One was in the evening, till closing time. The other was at lunchtime, when she went up to get the messages. And to steady herself, to face him.

Who knows where he got to? He had lots of things going on. All of us were dependent on him. Grainne—"Grainne's the pretty one," my mother would always say—was exceptionally smart and attractive and had jobs as personal assistant to various managing directors; this was as high as a young woman could expect to go in the world of work at the time. I—"Nuala's the brainy one," my mother would say—had temporary jobs and my scholarship was coming up. My next sister down, Deirdre—"Deirdre's the nice one," my mother would say, thus finishing off any general confidence the three of us might have had—was engaged to be married and had an office job. But emotionally we were in thrall to him. Then there were the brothers, always in difficulty or in trouble, then my little sisters and my youngest brother. None of them got much attention. But they were members not just of a family but of quite a self-consciously distinct—even a superior—family, all the same. My second-eldest brother used to be in the British army. He sits in a room in London, now, and drinks and reads. "I loved my mother and revered my father when I was a boy," he has written to me, in a letter that captures all our confusion.

They were Mother and Father, and does a child know any different? Sure it made me bed-wet when he came home pissed and pummelled my mother. Her cries for help were heartrending, and made me try to sleep in a chest of drawers. You didn't get to see Father much, but I loved him from afar.

The stranger would see my father's suave manners, his detachment, his humour, and think he was a modern type and that things must be lovely for us at home. And so they often were. He was usually delightful. And he was the head of the family, even if the family was going to ruin. His iron will created a version of a home life for himself. When he came in at night he would go out the back to the roses he grew and inspect them in the dark. He took his own clothes to the cleaners and polished his own shoes. He was invariably dapper and almost always cheerful. He whistled beautifully while he shaved. Nothing would have stopped him from surviving. He drove my mother into a frenzy.

"I've asked your mother to come to the Wexford Festival with me," he'd say airily—or to a garden party or a reception—"but she informs me she has nothing to wear. Isn't that so, Katherine? I gave you carte blanche to go into Brown Thomas—tell them to send the bill to me— and get something nice, but still, apparently, you claim you have nothing to wear." She choked with frustration, unable to find the words to say that she wasn't able to do things like that, and he knew it; that she had no good underwear or shoes, even if she had a dress; that she was too shy of shops to tell them to send bills; that one of the children was playing truant again; that he hadn't said how long they'd be going for, and who was supposed to be minding the house, and whether he'd give her the money for herself when they were there or she'd be waiting for him to buy drinks all the time—she was unable to say what she felt: that he was mocking her in her cage. She would be dying for him to get the hell out to work, so she could go up to the pub and get a quick double gin down her to stop the shaking.

But even his cruelty to her was not simple. A couple of times, when I went up to his bed to give him a message, I saw rosary beads under his pillow. He must have prayed by himself. He must have felt helpless, sometimes, under his apparent insouciance. During the next few years, when I was gradually getting away, the house—four bedrooms, eleven of us—vibrated with all the different individuals who lived there, each fighting to have some, at least, of their needs met. The clothes cupboard in the kitchen was a hopeless chaos of jumpers and socks, and sugar crunched underfoot in the kitchen. I brought home an English actor I had a crush on. No one had cleaned up the pools of tea on the table; soggy crusts lying in the cold tea looked like snails. "Good God!" he said. "It's like a set for an O'Casey tenement!"

At night the house was completely undefended. Gangs of boys used to come in the back door to the stairs that led to the bedrooms. They knew they could take liberties. There was no one there to care for my little sisters and brothers. My little sisters made a regular life for themselves. They put themselves to bed at nine. They tried to fix the clock to go off to get them to school on time. I remember the beds. My aunt's children often slept in Clontarf, too. There were so many of us that there were beds on the landing and in a windowless box-room. The bedclothes were supplemented by coats. There were only torn pieces of sheet— enough to put under your chin, to soften the rough coats. I do remember my mother pausing to fix a strip of cotton under some sleeping child's cheek. I never remember my father doing anything like that.

We all hated asking for money. I often stood on the landing outside my parents' bedroom trying to work up the courage to knock on the door and wake them to ask for it. Even when I was doing the entrance scholarship for UCD at Earlsfort Terrace, I had to get off the bus at the North Strand and walk the rest of the way because I hadn't the full fare. Yet we were not poor by the standards of the time. Many years later, I was interviewed on television by Anthony Clare, a broadcaster and psychiatrist, in a series about Irish people. I said I was poor when I was a student and, so as not to seem to be making exceptional claims for myself, I said that lots of people in UCD then were poor. The journalist Eamon Dunphy reviewed the series, and I've just tracked down his piece. "Watching Nuala O'Faolain depict herself as poor," he said, "I longed to kick the television set." He said, "Nuala's daddy was one of Ireland's most celebrated journalists, Terry O'Sullivan. Was she 'poor,' was 'everyone in UCD' poor? As anyone who was actually poor in the 1950s knows, the answer is no. No, no, no. In fact, nobody who went to UCD in those bleak years was poor. They were only playing at poverty." This is true, in a way. In the late 1950s, there were big marches of unemployed men in Dublin. They looked, and they were, desperate. They had no alternative to emigration.

But I was hurt, all the same. My father himself often didn't have a penny. And though the driver and the Austin Princess might occasionally be waiting for my little sisters at the gates of the National School when they came out, they might not have socks. They might not have copybooks. One of my little sisters had TB and lay around all the time. No one noticed, or, if they did, they did nothing. An older man friend of mine, a doctor, happened to call for me and he saw her languor. She spent a year in a sanatorium. Otherwise, I suppose, she would have died. My brothers, at that time, were the worst victims of the neglect that has left me with such an impression of poverty. They needed to be helped through school. But they never got through school. They were to stumble from one dead-end job to another. My friend the doctor and a Jesuit from Gardiner Street tried very hard to keep my eldest brother going towards the possibility of college. But they were defeated by my mother wanting him to earn money and my father washing his hands and pretending there was no problem. We were not poor. We had aspirations the really poor did not have; it wasn't strictly speaking because of money that we didn't attain them. I once heard about a Dublin journalist my own age who at that time was very poor. His mother was a maid in a hotel. The children would wait in the alleyway at the back of the hotel at night till she found out what bedroom was empty and smuggled them in. I envied him. I envy him that his mother took such care of them.

At the Fianna Fáil Christmas party for the press, the year Eamon Dunphy wrote that piece, I turned away from him. Charlie Haughey was Taoiseach then and ever the prime minister, he laughed at the two of us and made us shake hands. Back then, when we were poor inside our house but not outside, I used to drink with my parents in Groome's Hotel. I remember Charlie Haughey giving me a lift home from there once and settling down when he pulled up at the gate, and my mother coming out and rapping on the steamed-up glass of the car. Charlie Haughey and my father were very alike in a certain ironic grandeur of manner. They both came from modest backgrounds, and "Joey's" in Marino, where they both went to school, was no academy for the élite. Yet what a great time they were having in their prime! But my father was skating on thin ice. The bailiff often waited outside the house, propping himself on the wall of the shelter across the road. We survived from day to day. My brother's brilliant potential was ignored, and he went away on a merchant ship.

It wasn't possible to go to college from the house in Clontarf. It was too crisis-ridden. There was too much pain in it. But I didn't know that. I was proud of my family. You wouldn't often meet a man and woman as charming as my father and mother at even their half best. I was charmed by them. My mother made me her confidante. I listened to the details of my father's betrayals and her riposte: She was having a gauche little affair with a man in the pub. I didn't see the role my mother made me play—her confidante—as destructive. I thought I was living my own life. But when I got my scholarship I actually lost the money, lost the actual bank notes. This was exactly the kind of catastrophe I was used to.

On top of that, I didn't even go in to my first-year exam. I had become a supporter of Noel Browne's socialist group, and because I thought canvassing for it in a by-election was more important than my own life, I hadn't done any study. I remember my friend Nessa Boland begging me, at the main door of University College Dublin, to at least go into the hall, but I turned on my heel and walked out. I was drinking not only like, but often with, my "wild" aunt. I would never have got through the next years but for the older man, the doctor I had met at a Noel Browne meeting, who tried to keep an eye on me and all the family, and who saved me as certainly as he saved my sister with TB.

Because I was so involved with them, and because none of us had the slightest bit of insight into what we were doing, I almost sank with the sinking ship of the family. But luckily, I was pulled towards safety by the strong forces of love and sex. I was in town every night. I wanted my own place. I always worked part-time, and for a while I had a full-time job as a shopgirl in Boyer's department store and only went up to college to socialise. But my father didn't let me go without a struggle. There were repeated bitter rows. He'd slap my face one day and take me on a luxurious jaunt down the country to a race meeting or something the next. But I rented a bed-sitter, high up under the eaves, in Nassau Street. He called on me once, unexpectedly. When I opened the door he walked past without a word and went across to the sink and kicked the little tin I was using for rubbish out from under it, so that the tea leaves and peels went all over the floor. Then he ran down the stairs.

5

The outer boundaries of my experience when I was a student were, in one direction, literature and the people who were opening my mind to it, and, in the other direction, the business of love. Those were what mattered. I had confidence about the learning. One day I was idly listening to someone talk about Milton's sonnet "On His Blindness" and I suddenly understood the interrelation—and the third thing made by the interrelation—of form and content. This was a revelation almost as important as learning to read.

The English Department in UCD was just coming into the modern world then, at the end of the 1950s. Denis Donoghue introduced us to American poetry. To this day, the poems he showed us have a dimension of magic for me. He showed us Pound:

> *When, when, and whenever death closes our eyelids,*
> *Moving naked over Acheron*
> *Upon the one raft, victor and conquered together,*
> *Marius and Jugurtha together, one tangle of shadows.*

He showed us Wallace Stevens. He began with the beautiful conclusion to "Sunday Morning":

Deer walk upon our mountains, and the quail
Whistle about us their spontaneous cries.

He showed us Robert Frost:

She is as in a field a silken tent
At midday when a sunny summer breeze
Has dried the dew and all its ropes relent.

I remember those three poems in particular, because they fixed me in a preference for a magisterial tone in poetry. I find anything more friendly in lyric poetry not sufficiently grand.

Yet I had no confidence at all at the other boundary—at the business of love. Over the next few years, the few times I more or less went "all the way," it wasn't because I wanted to but because I was too shy about intimate things to talk about it. I didn't have the self-confidence to indicate "no." Or when it came up, wordlessly, the first time, I didn't have the words to say I didn't want to. Then, by doing it, I gained the confidence to say we should stop. This was the worst possible way of being with young men who were at least as confused as I was.

The boys and girls at University College Dublin, as far as I know, were prudish, and they often lived at home or in hostels run by priests and nuns, and they were prone—I was, anyway—to ambush by Catholic scruples. Honest randiness was not admitted, even by the students across Dublin at Trinity College, except by some wistful rugby types from Northern Ireland I somehow knew, who persisted in believing that Catholic girls were "easy." But even the older men at Trinity—men from Britain who had done National Service, or former servicemen from America—had to bow to the customs of quiet contraceptive-free Dublin. Drinking and talking and incessant going to the pictures were, among other things, sublimation.

There were different styles in lots of things between UCD and Trinity College. But a certain kind of person from either place—someone involved in theatre and drinking and literature—met on the shared ground of Grafton Street. "Oh, them, they're students," the middle-aged would say, because middle-aged men—the ones with money, in Jammet's and the Russell and the Shelbourne; the ones with artistic reputations, in McDaid's and the Bailey and O'Neill's—were the kings of the little city. I remember Dublin as dark and dramatic then, at the end of the 1950s, the streets drifting with smoke and rain. I see it in my mind's eye in black and white. Pubs and cafés were thrilling, because light and warmth spilled from them. The students moved like guerrillas around the centre of the city, hardly visible. They walked everywhere. They borrowed each other's coats. They lent each other books and ate egg-and-onion sandwiches and chips with mince sauce; if they had money, at three o'clock potato cakes came on the menu in Bewley's. You ate them slowly, a whole pat of butter on each one, sometimes accompanied by the snuffles of the satirist Myles na Gopaleen, toying with a sausage on toast at the next table.

Middle-aged or young, city people lived alone in cold bed-sitters that smelt of gas, with stained curtains and dripping bathrooms down lino-covered halls. There were hundreds of these lairs, with young men and women walking and getting buses from one to another. Even Trinity students, supposedly patrolled by proctors, could disappear into a network of rooms in Kenilworth Square and Waterloo Road and under pavement level in Leeson Street and up in the attics of Nassau Street and over the shops in Baggot Street. Couples went into the musty beds in the afternoons by silent agreement, she in her jumper and skirt and suspender belt, he pushing down his trousers under the blankets. The fumbles led to this and—ugh! ouch!—that; Buddy Holly serenading Peggy Sue on the Dansette record player so that the fellows playing cards next door wouldn't hear.

Everything I was learning was new to me. Caring about issues—De Valera's attempt to remove proportional representation, for example—was new. Politics was new. Nationalism was new. I had a boyfriend, that is to say, from a Tipperary Republican family who used to walk me up and down Molesworth Street while he plotted to blow up the Grand Lodge of the Freemasons—that was nationalism. Standing on O'Connell Bridge watching the unemployed men march and wondering whether anything could be done—that was politics. There was no party politics. It wasn't even that the Fianna Fáil party ran the country; De Valera, personally, ran the country.

Having friends was new. Learning from the enthusiasms of other people my own age was new. Knowing boys and men as companions was new. Not many people got to college thirty-odd years ago, and my fellow students, though often poor, were usually carefully raised. Most people left school at eleven, or fourteen, or after the Inter. They didn't get much of a chance to make friends of the opposite sex. They were meant to sense each other out at dances. That I did know about: the intensities in the laneways behind dance halls and coming out of the cinema with sore lips and swollen breasts. I did not know in any stable way how to behave. There was a cheap "invalid" wine then, called Vintara. I used to drink a lot of it. Onlookers, particularly if they had led sheltered lives, were appalled by how uninhibited it allowed a person to be.

It seemed to me that I was finished when I dropped out of UCD. Months of despair in London followed. I didn't even have the money to go to London, but that I took a job as a domestic in a hospital there. An agency in O'Connell Street paid your boat fare to that kind of job, the lowest of the low; then they took the money back out of your wages, so it was nearly impossible to save the fare home. I lived in a hostel near the hospital. I worked by myself in a basement room. There was a big tin machine that took dirty dishes in at one end and produced them at the other, a bit less dirty. I was in charge of that. I had been having a wonderful time at college. I'd had friends. Now I was so lonely in the evenings, lying on the bed, looking up at the window high in the wall, that my skin hurt. I tried not to think about Dublin, because all that was over, and as far as I knew for the rest of my life, I'd be some kind of an Irish worker in England. This experience of complete hopelessness went very deep. There were hardly any black people in England then, and no

Asians. The Irish and—more recently—Cypriots were the servant class. Down at my level you just lived to work to earn enough to live another week of work. I didn't see any way out.

An accident got me the fare back to Ireland. Lives were ruined at that time, thousands and thousands of them, quite casually, by the rules the patriarchy made for young women. They were hotly pursued, and half longed to yield, but they were not able to defend themselves against pregnancy, and they were destroyed if they got pregnant. I got the fare back to Ireland through one of those tragic pregnancies.

An Irishwoman I knew—a successful, well-dressed executive assistant who normally wouldn't have mixed with me—thought she might be pregnant. She came to me and we went to a doctor. She took off her jumper and bra and he just peered at her and said yes, she was pregnant. He said it coldly. She paid him. Outside, it was a winter night. She held on to the wall, dry-eyed, trying to grasp the ruin that faced her. Almost the worst thing was: How would she tell her parents? In the end, I was given the fare to go back to Ireland to tell them, while she waited in London to hear how they took it.

That was how I got back to Dublin.

This young woman had barely begun her life when pregnancy struck her. But that is her story, for her to tell. All I know is that she hid out in Belfast and that I was there with her for the last few days before the baby was born. We walked around all the time, aimlessly, because we had no money to go in anywhere. I saw her a few hours after the birth, weeping in her bed, her milk seeping through the bandages she was tightly bound with. Her father came up from Dublin, and he and I were the only people in a side chapel when a priest baptised the baby. Then I took the baby to the train for Dublin. In Dublin I got a bus to a suburb. I handed the baby in to the nun in a home there, to be kept until it was adopted. All that way, the baby never cried. I didn't know until many years later that the mother used to go out to that home and look through the hedge at the children's playtime, in the hope of seeing a child who looked like herself.

And still I was having unprotected sex myself. I didn't know how to get out of having sex. I never thought of the man as having a responsibility to me. Though now I don't forgive the older man, for instance, who took me on a holiday to Connemara, which I'd never seen before, when I was nineteen. This man was Irish, but he had been travelling abroad. He was the first travelled man I ever knew, and I revered him for his knowledge. I felt I had to sleep with him to keep him interested in me. But I only knew how to court. I remember him bending over my naked body—I hated it being out in the open—in the bed in the damp cottage we'd had to pretend to be married to get (I wore the twist of gold paper from a cigarette packet as a ring when I met the landlady). He was pulling at the hair under my arm, as a sort of playful initiatory move. "Relax," he ordered. "Come on, come on!" he urged me. "Be a bit more relaxed, can't you?" But I was coldly embarrassed by him. We sat on cliff tops in the windy sunshine and he told me about his sex life. I was supposed to be inducted into adult sensuality by his confidences. I sat in the glass porch of the little hotel near the cottage and read my way through back copies of *The New Yorker*, grimly putting in the time till I could get away from the holiday and from him.

This man later wrote me a letter about what "a man" wants from "a woman." I enter it here as a document from patriarchal times:

Dear Little Sister,

You can give him (by "him" I mean the man you will want to give to) first of all companionship. You can be the sieve for his ideas and his enthusiasms, the moderator of his superfluous angers, the soft bosom of his hard days, his scourge to action—or his dangler of promised sweetmeats—when he slackens. You will give him the freedom of loving you exclusively. You will tie him to this stern, sweet discipline, let him feel the demands of your love. For he lives only as a shadow-man if his heart can know no outpouring, his selfishness no merciless self-destruction, if his countless good impulses and scattered loves have no single gathering-point and centre where they realise themselves and have meaning. You will give him this—you will give him the manly task of earning your love again daily. You will give him the delight of his eyes when he looks at you bright and neat and clean, when he notices yet once again that your eyes heed him. You will give all these things to him no matter how strong or wise or world-famous he may be. And when you make the gift of yourself, please let it be with humble awareness of all these things which you are giving—that's what will make your gift very rich and meaningful. You are right to prize highly "interesting people," brain knowledge and the world of books and to seek after them. But I have told you the things your man will want from you. Believe me.

This ineffable letter—particularly the veiled threat at the end about a man (him) not wanting a woman (me) to go seeking after knowledge and books and so on—ranks in its small way with Mr. Collins's proposal in *Pride and Prejudice* as a piece of perfectly unqualified egotism.

In those years, sex only made sense to me once. I was friendly with an American man who was doing a postgraduate degree in Dublin. He was much older than the rest of us—he'd been in the CIA, even, according to himself. He had the records of *West Side Story* and a paperback of J. D. Salinger's stories. He shared a basement apartment in Waterloo Road with a lot of other men. One afternoon when I went round there, he was the only person in. We flirted around on the bed in his room, not very seriously. Then the doorbell rang and he went off down the passage to answer it. He came back in, and with his face all screwed up, and feeling his way blindly, and without a word, he pushed and pulled my clothes apart and forced himself into me. After a few awful minutes of red-hot pain he collapsed onto my shocked body, sobbing dreadfully. He sat on the edge of the bed after a while and put his head in his hands. "That was a telegram," he said. "My mother is dead."

• • •

I did, after a year of near desperation, get back into college. The writer Mary Lavin—whose fondness for me was one of my strokes of luck—gave me an allowance for six weeks, to study to redo the exams. I had exactly enough for a room in Pembroke Street and a chip supper—which I thought about all day—in Cafolla's of Baggot Street Bridge. Then when I got back in to UCD, I had no scholarship, so I couldn't pay the fees. But the Jesuit in Gardiner Street who was told about me by my doctor friend gave me the fees—a sum I could never have hoped to get for myself. Eventually I won a minor prize and, along with having jobs all the time, I got through to my degree. Not without constant trouble with the college authorities: I was reported to them, for example, for "unbecoming behaviour" at a party—Vintara-induced behaviour. But I was also kindly helped by UCD, especially the women who ran the front office. I loved the place. I love the memory of every room and corridor of it.

I was twenty when I met Michael. My mother said, "Are you sure you love him?" "Oh, Mammy," I said. I was at the end of her bed, and she had put down her book and pushed her specs down her nose because this interested her, "Oh, Mammy, I'll die if I can't see him. I'll die!" I had bumped into him a few weeks earlier on the steps of the National Library. I saw him lifting his face to the sun there—the curve of his cheekbones, the shadows of his eyelashes. I knew him slightly; I'd borrowed his cottage on a hill near Dublin once. Now the cottage gave us something to talk about while we stood—in the middle of a crowd in a bona fide pub outside Dublin—like poles connected by a high-tension cable. Going back into town in someone's packed car I sat on his lap. We hardly breathed. "I'll ring you" was as much as he could say when they dropped me, and I just swallowed and walked away.

He rang. "Come down to the cottage on Saturday"—as-it-were lightly. "You know the way. We can go for a walk, have a bit of supper." But it was the winter. Snow started falling. Then a blizzard set in. By Saturday morning there were drifts, even in Dublin. All the main roads were closed. There was no chance of the bus going. He had no phone at the cottage. And even if he had—I didn't want a new arrangement! I had to have this one! I had been living for this one! I was asking my mother to give me the train fare to the nearest station. "But how far is the station from the cottage?" "I don't know, Mammy, but if I can just get there I'll get to the cottage somehow." Mammy got out of bed and looked in her coat pockets and her bag and gave me all the money she had.

Down the country the snow had stopped falling. It was a still, glassily cold winter afternoon. The sky was palest yellow. A few cars had been along the road from the station earlier and made deep ruts in the snow. Now the ruts hurt my feet as I crunched along, because the rough edges of snow had frozen again. I had ordinary shoes on; I wouldn't let him see me in rubber boots. The road went into the woods, and snow sifted down from the branches and trickled down the inside of my polo neck and spread across my back. A man in a car going not much faster than I was gave me a lift. I was so numb that I could not pull the door of the car towards me. He was worried about me, when I said to drop me where a lane went up to the cottage. It was getting dark. "I'm fine," I said, "and my friend is just up the road!" I didn't want to be delivered to the cottage with a fuss. I had to seem casual.

But when I crunched through the snow and up to the door of the cottage, red-faced with exertion and shyness and anticipation, Michael wasn't there. The fire was still warm. But he had gone—inching his way, no doubt, to Dublin.

I cried. Then I took the lamp I had lit, balancing its glass chimney carefully before me as I climbed the steep wooden stairs. I took off my skirt and stockings and got into what must be his bed. I had a last miserable cigarette, and the blankets gradually warmed up and I went asleep.

Sometime later I woke at the sound of the bedroom door opening. He stood there. The lamp was still lighting. He was quite unable to say anything, or smile, and neither was I. Then he came into bed and his warm arms rolled me on top of him, so that my mouth was exactly positioned where we could be at ease. And sometime that night, not moving much, he melted into me and moved me with all my assent, up and down, in and out. And in the end, I lay in the crook of his shoulder, new-minted. So that was it! That was what it had all been about! I got to know every detail of that bedroom. That night, the frost would have filmed the diamond panes of the little window beside the bed, but where one pane was cracked the glass was always clear. I would have seen the stars through it.

From then on, Michael was my man, though the "my" sounds more assured than it ever was. But I was still a student and a Dubliner, whereas he lived in the country, mostly, reading and playing the piano. He took no interest in the society we were part of. Not many people did. Noel Browne's socialist party had ended in an impassioned meeting in Moran's Hotel, where the various personalities split. I remember David Thornley, the leader of the dissident faction, stumbling down from the stage, crying. The big bitter marches of the late 1950s against emigration and poverty and hunger had long since stopped—the Archbishop got the leaders good jobs, was what was said. The Republic had settled into being a one-party state. In the early 1960s I knew more about Welsh politics than Irish ones. I had long had a crush on a Welsh nationalist, and when I'd gone to see him in Wales I had stood transfixed in Woolworth's in Bangor, because the shopgirls spoke Welsh. I had never heard ordinary working-class people speaking anything but English. I'd been to Mass with him in an upstairs room: it was more like glamorous, embattled early Christianity than the huge ordinary churches of Dublin. I stayed for a while on a Welsh nationalist farm. I read the texts of Welsh cultural nationalism like Saunders Lewis's *Why We Burnt the Bombing School*, and I had a Welsh phrase book I studied. When I went with the Welshman to the currach races on Galway Bay I dimly noticed Irish-speaking Ireland. But I had no interest in Irish. Of course, this says little or nothing about the Ireland of the time. No doubt if I had had a crush on a Connemara man, I'd be a fluent speaker now.

Nevertheless, it was a feature of the intellectual life—if that is not too grand a word for it—of the Dublin I knew then that it wasn't interested in the condition of Ireland. Nothing was happening. Northern Ireland was a far-off place. When Edna O'Brien's first books came out they were a catalyst for women to exchange confidences, and I learnt that quite a few people went to Belfast to get condoms. Condoms, hats, cheap butter: That was the extent of it. *The Bell* magazine had no successor of the same importance. Things were happening in England. Artists seemed to have more money in England; they could hardly have had less than the Dublin ones. I often stayed in the basement in Leeson Street (now, surreally, a nightclub) where the poet Leland Bardwell and her children lived, which was also an after-closing-time salon and a dosshouse for people with no beds to go to. It was a centre for English and Scottish poets and painters who drifted across from Soho to see Leland—or Anthony Cronin, who was a key figure in the literary life of the time as an editor and a writer himself. Maybe at the level of Anthony Cronin, contemporary Ireland was under discussion. But I was just a student, and perhaps the only student of my generation who never wrote a poem or a story.

Otherwise, there were poets everywhere. And essayists. Erudite young men like Owen Dudley Edwards wrote essays for small magazines or to deliver to student societies. Everyone tried to convert other people to admiration for this or that writer or historical figure. This was at a time when feature journalism was completely undeveloped. Ideas and information were on their first time around. So when Owen talked about Swift, say, or Parnell and Kitty O'Shea, or Housman's life and poetry, or Sherlock Holmes, it was all new.

I began to write small items for Radio Éireann; the broadcaster Sean Mac Réamoinn got me the work. I'd bring my scripts in to him in the studio in Henry Street, tripping down the long passage with its coconut-matting runner, and in one of the glass doors whose function was lettered in gold in an Irish replete with *fadas* and *seimhiús*. He'd run his pencil through the first paragraph; then, when we started broadcasting, I'd hear my first paragraph recycled as his introduction. Then he might

take me across to the Tower Bar. He was a wellspring of enthusiasms—
for Christianity, crosswords, chess, women, Celtic literature, food,
jaunts down the country in someone's rare car. Rural Ireland was far
away in every way, then. The *Fleadh Cheoil*—traditional music gather-
ings held in country towns—were just beginning to make an impact, and
the soundtrack of the film *Mise Eire* left audiences rapt. But before I met
Sean I had never known anyone to have a recording of Irish music. *My
Fair Lady* I remember being passed around, but never Irish music.

Ideas were transmitted by talking. Student magazines mattered, and
student societies, and what was said at them. There was a very severe eye
kept, in UCD, on guest speakers. But soon after I went to college a paper
somehow slipped the net, on religions of the Mediterranean basin. I got
such a shock listening to it that I remember now the big oval mahogany
table we were all sitting at, in a room just off the main hall in Earlsfort
Terrace. I had hardly heard the word "religion" used in the plural before. No one had ever told me that trinities and virgin mothers and
deaths and resurrections were known in places other than Christianity. I
was still a practising Catholic then, and I was very seriously shaken. I
had taken it for granted that the alternatives were to be a good Catholic
or a bad Catholic. My education had not prepared me for not believing
at all. When I had my own first piece published, it was about the visual
references to the Via Dolorosa in Bergman's *Wild Strawberries*. This was
a real period topic—the few foreign films that came to Dublin were scru-
tinised up and down. And the Irish Catholic version of Christianity was
more or less the only world system we knew anything about ourselves.
We had been trained to read events—Hungary, the Bay of Pigs—in the
light of their anti- or pro-Catholicism. The first stirrings of intellectual
life, after school, were likely to involve trying to assimilate the new
thing, whatever it might be, to the familiar religion.

There was an unself-conscious interest in ideas. A friend might send
you a note to say that you absolutely must meet in Hartigan's; they'd had
an idea for a short story. Someone was trying to take plays from Player's
in Trinity to Edinburgh, and, in both UCD and Trinity, French drama

was having a passing currency. Claudel and Camus were grist to the mill of Irish youth. We student theatre types would try anything: Beckett's *All That Fall* was a perfect success, but a Strindberg one-acter was abandoned when the audience burst into hysterical laughter at the line, "I saw your feet in the bathhouse and ever since I have loved you." I put on a dire production of *The Lower Depths*, not least because Moscow subsidised publications like Gorky's *Plays*, and you could get copies in the Communist bookshop in Dublin very cheaply. If you had an enthusiasm, you shared it. Paddy Connolly, later to be Attorney General, knew all about Wagner. My friend Eithne O'Neill wrote to me (in Irish and French—she was practising her languages) about the stories of Doris Lessing. Nabokov was passed from reader to reader. Two students had a plan to put on *Volpone* under the pillars of the portico of the General Post Office as some kind of statement about neo-classicism. When you discovered something it was like winning a prize, and you went out to share it. John Montague's poem "All Legendary Obstacles," I remember, was like that. Reading it for the first time was an event in one's life.

Leland read everything and passed everything on. Her musty basement in Leeson Street was a most various place. It could be frightening. All the usual inhabitants decamped from McDaid's pub one night and went to see the comedian Jimmy O'Dea in *Mother Goose*, the pantomime that Christmas. My friend Laila, an elegant Egyptian, baby-sat Leland's baby. He was no trouble—he drank his milk from a Gordon's Gin bottle with a teat and went asleep. But Laila was reading Poe, and the shadows seemed to gather around her. She grabbed the baby and spent the hours out on the step. Then again, the basement was sometimes a bridge school. Leland comes of Protestant stock and she has her accomplishments. She was a bridge player and horse rider. She did keep a horse, when the Corporation rehoused her in Tallaght: her neighbours called her a tinker. Leland was as poor as my mother had ever been, and she was perfectly capable of having as many babies. Yet she survived and helped other people to survive. She was the support system for a generation of writers, down in her basement, stirring a stew with one hand

and comparing translations of Baudelaire, as it might be, with the other. Her head was stocked. In a note to me in London from the writer Dermot Healy in Cavan, maybe ten years later, he remarks:

> Leland was just unbelievably good on the radio these past few Saturdays. A mixture of French singing, Mozart, Paul Durcan, and her father. "Isn't that lady's voice beautiful," the girl said in the pub where I was listening. And when I returned this Saturday she switched over immediately to Radio Éireann. The gypsies who occupy the pub nodded approval. They congratulated me when my own name was mentioned: "Very nice, mister, very nice indeed."

Bohemia was where women and men were closest, in those days when the sexes were such strangers. But there was no equality. I once ventured to ask Leland why she was with a particular man, who was unpleasant to her. "Who else would I get?" she said. "At my age?" Yet she was still young enough to be having babies.

You could not, then, in the Dublin of the 1960s, just go and live openly with your lover. Formally, Michael and I did not live together. Even my mother only accepted the situation because we were going to get married as soon as we could. (He had been married in England, but he and his wife had not been living together for some time. Divorces took a few years, then.) I spent a night with him once in a notoriously free-thinking boardinghouse in Rathgar. When I came out in the morning, a carload of men, who had been waiting, crawled along beside me as I walked away. Leaning out, they half threatened me and half pleaded with me to go home like a good girl and go to Confession. They were Catholic vigilantes. My patron—the doctor who had helped me and the family over and over again—went to my professor of Old English, a priest, to ask him to use his influence to stop me seeing Michael. (No one expected anything of my parents.) The house Michael lived in was full of secret liaisons like ours, because the houses where unmarried couples were known to be tolerated weren't very many. The girl in the front room was visited every evening by a young man who lived with his mother in Fitzwilliam Square. They were actually married, but no one knew.

I was never part of my original family again. But their address was my permanent address: unmarried daughters lived at home, in principle, if they lived in the same town. Bed-sitter Dublin had different rules from today's apartment-block Dublin. The only definite break came if you married and had children yourself. Girls and boys married each other then who would have a passing relationship now: Michael and I would have married within the first few months if he hadn't been married already. I thought he was wonderful. He was very good-looking. Sometimes I could hardly breathe because he was near me. And he knew about music. I listened to music in his room all one summer. He had a big pile of records: Clara Haskil playing Mozart, Bartók, Chopin, Walton, Telemann, Bach. He read in French and Italian. He looked after himself. He loved the outdoors, whereas I had hardly ever even been for a walk. He drank very little, disliked smoking, and he prepared fresh vegetarian food. This was the last straw for my mother. "Don't you think he's a bit dull, dear?" she'd say, when I went out to the pub she drank in to see her.

He was in every way a good influence on me. (What if I had discovered orgasm with a person as reckless as myself?) He took me abroad for a holiday at a time when there wasn't even a concept of "holidays." Most young people always needed to work; I was a lunchtime waitress and had to keep the job. There was no television and no travel material in newspapers. In the circumstances, even the bland British travelogues which came on before the main picture in cinemas—sunny Bournemouth, a flower festival on Jersey—were exotic. By the time I was twenty-one, I had only been to three or four places in Ireland, and nowhere else except the hellhole of London and to Paris, when I was at school and won a French government essay competition. I had never eaten in an outdoor restaurant. I had hardly ever seen a black person and never spoken to one. So when Michael took me to join his friends on a boat on the

Mediterranean, I was aching with readiness to travel. The overnight train went down through France. As dawn came up, I saw for the first time, from the rattling, hot, cindery-smelling compartment, vineyards, sunflowers, quilts hung out of windows. That first night we stayed in a high room in a once-ornate pension somewhere in the dense alleyways between the station and the port in Genoa. We went out into the crowd and the noise. The air was pungent. Bright prostitutes sat on kitchen chairs at the corners of the streets. There was a smell of smoke, a vision of great church doors, children chasing each other, people haggling and shouting and laughing, and a big smooth rat who made his way along the side of a wall. We went down a step into an earth-floored café and saw a pizza oven for the first time, and, as I was to do for a long time, I ate just vegetable soup because at least it had potatoes in it.

Another time we went on a motorbike through France. Every mile of the journey—before we puttered down the other side of the Alps, amazed at the soldiers holding hands in the dark park in Aosta—is still vivid. Like the bookish provincials we were, we went to Rouen, to the Flaubert museum in a pavilion in his garden. There was a little greyish cloth under a glass dome. This was the handkerchief, the card said, with which Flaubert "*a essuyé son front, quelques instants avant sa mort.*" We went to Nevers, because in the movie *Hiroshima Mon Amour*—which had reduced myself and Laila to abject, quivering rapture—the Marguerite Duras character keeps saying, "*Je rappelle Nevers.*" We went to Autun and looked at the Ghislebertus tympanum; Iris Murdoch had used the serpent in that carving as a symbol of evil in her latest book.

But in real life, after I got my degree, I was stuck again. Then a professor from UCD—Robin Dudley Edwards—came all the way out to my parents' house in Clontarf, where I was living, with a message from my own Old English professor. There was a scholarship in Medieval English being offered by the University of Hull. It was only a small scholarship, but there was nothing coming up in Ireland for another two years. My patron, the doctor, bought me a suit and a ticket to Hull for an interview, and I got that scholarship.

In Hull, that winter of 1961, the skies were grey streaked with black. The wind sliced in from the North Sea. In a launderette once, a Ghanaian man urgently showed me photos of his wife and children in Africa. He wept. No one could do anything about the loneliness of postgraduate students. They'd come from warm, peopled lives to a place with no reward except scholarship. I was no scholar. I began to wither. I went to tea—scones, marble cake—every Sunday on a rota of Christian families organised by the Anglican padre. I went to a double bill of *The Rake's Progress* and *Don Pasquale*. I went to an Irish event:

> The dancing will consist of Ceilidhe Dancing and Old Time Waltzes. There will also be songs and request items. We look forward to your continued interest in this very necessary effort. St. Enda's club has the formal approval and blessing of His Lordship, the Bishop of Middlesbrough.

Michael had got work as an extra in a film sometime previously, and when the film—*The World of Suzie Wong*—came to Hull, I sat all day in a freezing cinema, waiting for the moment when you could see his head come around again.

I had wanted to try to be independent. But I couldn't stand the loneliness. Michael came over and we pretended to be married and got a flat on a grey suburban street. We lay in front of the gas fire reading Flaubert's letters. We went south, across the flat plains of eastern England, and I thought his eyes were exactly the same colour as the roof of Lincoln Cathedral after rain. That was the sort of thing I thought, even if I didn't say, when I was twenty-one.

At the end of one year at Hull I took the risk of coming back to Dublin, to work towards getting the big Irish scholarship that paid for you to study anywhere in the world you chose. Not that it was all that urgent to go on studying. Michael and I would be getting married, wouldn't we? Just as soon as he got his divorce.

6

Years after I was in Hull, the poet Philip Larkin apologised. "I was asked to look out for you," he said. "But I'm afraid I couldn't be bothered." It is a pity he didn't bother. We could have discussed, if all else failed, his state-of-the-art library at the university, which I sincerely admired. I would have been happy, tucked into the stacks, reading the publications of the Early English Texts Society, if I hadn't missed Michael so much. "I did see you coming in and out of the library," Larkin said to me, "but you seemed all right." This was at lunch in a hotel in Cheltenham, ten years later. I was working for the BBC making Open University programmes, and I was making one about poetry and television and the problems associated with supplying images for a poem. I wanted to record him reading his own poem, "Here," for the sound track. Normally, he didn't do that kind of thing. But because he remembered my name with a little guilt, he asked me to join himself and his mother in Cheltenham, where he would read the poem into my tape recorder.

Thus I had one of the more disconcerting meals of my life. Both the Larkins seemed to be somewhat deaf. And the hotel lounge we had pre-lunch drinks in, and then the dining room itself, had a tin roof. It was raining very hard, so it was difficult to hear in any event. Philip would say something like "Another gin and tonic, Mother?" and Mrs. Larkin would reply with something like "I must say I agree with you about the fish" and I'd say something like "What amazingly heavy rain," and Philip would say "Certainly, I'll just catch the waiter's eye." We got through an extremely boozy lunch at these gentle cross-purposes. Then he and I went out the back, the two of us and the tape recorder squashed under his big black umbrella. There was a stone-built shed there, where the staff kept their bicycles. We were away from traffic and people. We sat on a low wall, companionably, and he started off:

> *Swerving east, from rich industrial shadows*
> *And traffic all night north; swerving through fields*
> *Too thin and thistled to be called meadows*
> *And now and then a harsh-named halt, that shields*
> *Workmen at dawn . . .*

He was a wonderful reader, and a most attractive man, sending out both a nonthreatening message and a message about being more threatening than his nonthreatening image made him appear.

I've known a lot of writers on that kind of anecdotal level. I digress, and mention some of them, though I was never reverent about writing, myself. My father, after all, wrote, in his way, as the daily bread-winning task. People I lived with wrote, banging away oblivious to me, often when I wanted them to do other things. I never even read what they produced—I was exceptionally uninterested in anything by anyone I knew myself. It wasn't until I presented the *Booklines* programme on Irish television that I ever asked any writer about writing. This wasn't always easy. The living short-story writer I most admire, Alice Munro, told me that as a young woman in remote Ontario she'd read and been inspired by Mary Lavin, which was very pleasing. But when it came to her own writing and I started interviewing her in the studio, she leaned away from me, her fine eyes looking at me warily, as if I'd gone slightly mad— as if she couldn't think why I was asking her all these crazy questions.

Some kinds of writers, I thought afterwards, don't want to know their own methods.

But some kinds of writing are almost as interesting to talk about as to read. I directed an interview with Norman Mailer about *An Executioner's Song*, and I interviewed him myself about *Harlot's Ghost*; both interviews, it seemed to me, were legitimate, if tiny, offspring of the books. I interviewed Kingsley Amis in a very small hotel room in Kensington, and afterwards we knocked back duty-free whiskey and Amis was like a big, pink, particularly likable baby. I directed an interview with John Betjeman, and he gave us all champagne and pined for Anglo-Irish demesnes we Irish television people had never heard of. Seamus Heaney was always a selfless promoter of poets and poetry, which is one of the reasons the Nobel prize was so rightly given to him. If he agreed to talk about poetry on television, he prepared for the task. And he always found a way to be meaningfully generous. I remember, particularly, the way he talked about Derek Mahon's poetry (Derek Mahon himself could not be lured by any bribe whatsoever to appear in front of a camera). In Princeton, Joyce Carol Oates turned out to be an enthusiast for Roddy Doyle. In London, we had supper with Eileen O'Casey in an Italian restaurant, and although she was in her eighties she enslaved the waiters with her charm.

In interviews you do get a glimpse of personality. But mostly it is rote work for the writers, though few of them recycle themselves with quite the same economy as J. B. Priestley, whom I met once at a dinner party in London—delighted to meet him, because I'd read his *Bright Day* over and over when I was a child. Priestley amused the dinner table with an improvisation about being on holiday in Ireland recently and noticing that Irish girls have lovely hair but terrible legs. Flying to Dublin a few days later, I picked up the in-flight magazine. It hadn't been an improvisation. There was an article by J. B. Priestley: "Irish girls have lovely hair but terrible legs," it began.

I have a friend who is a very successful novelist—David Lodge. He's thought of, now, as a comic writer. But I loved about him, from the moment I met him, a sombre scrupulousness—of which his English Catholicism is part—which may be the ground of the comic necessity in him, but which makes the person (as often happens with writers) the very opposite of the author. The only writer who looked and behaved like "a writer" all the time (and who I ever felt I worked with in a collaborative sense) was John Berger. This was when I was making television programmes for the arts faculty of the Open University. Zola's *Germinal* was one of the texts on the course on the nineteenth-century novel, and to do something about that novel, for the television component of the course, the professor of English wanted his old socialist comrade. John Berger was an art critic and novelist who had just had a great success on television with a series about the social role of paintings called *Ways of Seeing*. It was going to be difficult to get him to agree to do an Open University programme, and the professor and I flew to Geneva to try to talk him into it. It took a whole evening. John's wife mostly moved around the room, preparing a meal and doing things quietly with the children.

Things went stiffly at first. But a photograph of Zola's overstuffed sitting room, in his villa near Paris, led to inspiration. It suggested to John something about the limits of the material. There is a gap between what you can feel and see and what you can imagine. Zola, as bourgeois as his furniture on one level, could articulate what to the bourgeoisie is a nightmare vision of coal miners, because they cannot see them. They imagine them, deep under the ground, menacing, formlessly, as the rise of the proletariat menaces the bourgeoisie. The argument wasn't linear; I only ever grasped its possible shape when John would turn his beautiful face to mine and earnestly go over it. But the programme wasn't just an illustration of an argument—that was what was creative about it. We went to Derbyshire and filmed, with immense difficulty, down a coal mine. We filmed life aboveground and life underground, and John talked about the gap between, and I freeze-framed images of people in the village and unfroze them and used a brass band playing Gounod's *Mors et*

Vita on the sound track. We made a film about the life in darkness. In general we thought we had been richly suggestive, rather than prescriptive. And perhaps we had been.

It was a wonderful experience, working with him and knowing him, at that particular time. His novel *G* had just won the Booker Prize, and he was in the process of giving half his prize money to the Black Panthers and was always taking taxis to Caribbean clubs in the Finsbury Park direction. And he was writing poems; he gave me some. He took me around a bit. I adored him. And he thought I was very gifted. When we were filming at the coal mine he used to hold me at night because it was very difficult work and I couldn't sleep from anxiety. "Think about Donegal," he used to say. "Think of the waves on the shore in Donegal." I didn't like to admit that he'd got it generously wrong. I wasn't from glamorous Donegal; I was only from County Dublin.

I mention this as an epitaph, almost, on unconsciousness. I was lost in hero worship. I never gave a thought to his then wife—a brilliant woman—or the children, back in Geneva. He was above all that, I would have said. No one is above anything, she implied, in a piece she published in the feminist magazine *Spare Rib* not long after. It was an account—a deadpan, detailed account—of cleaning the inside and the outside of a lavatory.

Philip Larkin had been asked to mind me in Hull, when I went there in 1961, by Patricia Avis, who lived with Professor Desmond Williams of UCD, who later had a small dalliance with me. (We'd meet in London at ⸱ the Ritz or with his *Daily Telegraph* friends in The King and Keys in Fleet Street. He was said to be on MI5 work, but mysteries were his stock-in-trade.) Patricia Avis had written two books. Charles Monteith of Faber wouldn't publish the first because, according to the poet Richard Murphy, who was for a time her husband, "it slandered his friends." I wish I'd known that when I was seated beside a gushing Charles Monteith at a dinner in All Souls, four or five years after Hull. I wish I could have told him what I think of such lethal arrogance.

She died—alcohol and pills—with no hope of either book being published. Yet by all accounts, she was as clever as the clever men—Kingsley Amis, Conor Cruise O'Brien, Larkin—she knew. I see articles about her that imply she was a doomed soul. That's an argument often used to cover up indefensible circumstances. She was nearly in time for the breakout—for getting support from other women, getting published by women's presses, and so forth. But when she was in her prime, writing and publishing was a man's world.

Though exceptional women could survive. One I knew personally was Mary Lavin, who so kindly helped me try to get back into college. Mary did not frequent pubs. But she was not a housewife, either. She had a town house and a country house and used hotels. She had the status of the respectable widow she was. She also had a great love. But the loved one, handily, did not impinge on her daily life, since he was a Jesuit and usually in Australia. She had money and health and three daughters who interested her enormously. She could run things her way. Above all, she had been an only child, adored and affirmed by her father. When I knew her, she treated her widowed mother with harassed affection, as if her mother were her least favourite child.

But I did not know, when I was a young woman, a functioning wife or mistress who wrote. Most of them were too poor to be able to spare the time. Patricia Avis was wealthy, but though that might have helped her write her novels, it didn't (in her lifetime) get them published. It wasn't in the mind of girls to write. The young writers at Mary Lavin's house were all men; the women were all women who were going out with the men. If you were a young female, no one asked you what you did, around the pubs of Dublin, or what you wanted to do. They assessed you in terms of themselves. You were welcome if you fitted in. The "literary Dublin" I saw lied to women as a matter of course and conspired against the demands of wives and mistresses. Outside the home, in the circles where academics and journalism and literature met, women either had to make no demands, and be liked, or be much larger than life, and feared. It wasn't at all easy to be formidable and also desirable. Patricia Avis was like a zombie with misery. I saw Maire Mac an tSaoi in the corner of an obscure pub once, in urgent talk with a man. She would have been the exception, but she wrote in Irish.

For a while when I was a student I lived on Leland's sofa, under a pile of coats, in one corner of the big front room, and the poet Patrick Kavanagh had a bed on the other side. He was a terrible flatmate. He coughed and hawked and tramped, muttering, out into the area under the steps and pissed copiously and often, groaning and talking to himself while he did. His heartburn was not helped by his starting to drink again each morning, as soon as an inventory of his pocket and mine, and of the number of bottles that could be returned and their deposits retrieved, had established the day's opening budget.

He was too wrapped up in the struggle to keep himself going to take any notice of extraneous people. That's how it was possible to share a room with him. But though he was usually curmudgeonly, he took the trouble to amuse when he was feeling well and had a few bob. And his health did get better—or didn't get worse at the speed you would have expected—over the years. The worst kind of end, which seemed to be lying in wait for him, was fended off, because his woman friend, Katherine Moloney, began to look after him. I used to meet him, a few years after sharing the basement in Leeson Street, in London, in a pub opposite the British Museum. He wasn't just better physically; he was in better humour than he had been in Dublin. Katherine lived in London, and she minded him. (Misogyny is so ingrained in some quarters that this important fact is overlooked.) I remember him positively entertaining the company once with tales of the millionairess's castle in Italy he'd just been staying in. "My hostess invented the brassiere," he rasped, startling the strangers around in the Museum Tavern. "That's what made Caresse Crosby rich. The brassiere did." He'd obviously been patronising Italian shops; he was eating straight *Bicarbonato di Soda* from a big packet. He went off with Katherine that night as spry as anything. And he wasn't impossible the day he and Katherine were married in Dublin. Eoin and Joan Ryan—I was always told that Joan was the woman the poet is grieving in the poem "Raglan Road"—gave the wedding meal in their house in Leeson Park. There was a big table, covered in dishes, and lots of drink. Patrick looked a bit remote. But then, many of the guests were out of their element. There were people there who had never seen each other except in pubs, or flats that were extensions of pubs.

Paddy's presence was always the weightiest in any company he was in. But that was because of his self—the difficulty, if not impossibility, of engaging his attention, much less of charming him, unless he chose. If he did choose, the attention he directed at a person could be surprisingly warm and simple, behind his awkwardness. His personality would have compelled attention, even if he had been less of a writer.

Writing in itself was not revered in literary Dublin. A lot of people wrote, and no bones were made about it. It was not thought of as a raid on the inarticulate, or anything like that, so much as a craft that you might keep yourself by practising. It was something anyone might be engaged in. When I was around Dublin in the early 1960s I might call in to the National Library to see Mary Lavin. She wrote there, and in the foyer of Buswell's, and on a breadboard sitting up in her bed in Bective in the early morning, before she got her daughters up for school. Round in McDaid's, the novelist John Broderick might be getting ready to go home to Athlone, where his business was writing. Down in the Stag's Head, the playwright Tom McIntyre might be talking about writing with playwright Tom Kilroy, who was writing. Myles na Gopaleen might be in Neary's, not talking to anyone. (I spent an evening there once with poet Louis MacNeice and the two men didn't address each other.) The novelist Ben Kiely might be in the White Horse on Burgh Quay, hypnotizing some young woman with his talk. My friend Sean Mac Réamoinn might be in the Tower Bar with a visiting writer, like Anthony Burgess. Liam O'Flaherty might be walking home along the canal.

I knew the novelist John McGahern for a few years. We shared a Northside home ground, me in Clontarf, he in his digs on the Howth Road. We met in high dim pubs at the bottom of the Malahide Road or further down Fairview. "I work much," he wrote to me—we wrote and sent telegrams across Dublin in those days, because there were no private phones at bed-sit level—"so much I hate the sight of a white page. I'll send you my work sometime. I think about you in some of it." He had already written *The Barracks* when I met him. We used to go to the pictures a lot—the five o'clock show, because he was well out of Belgrove School, where he taught, by five—followed by a snack in an O'Connell Street ice-cream parlour. We were in an ice-cream parlour when he showed me the telegram from Faber and Faber that accepted *The Barracks* for publication with the greatest enthusiasm.

As I recall, John was recovering from pain connected with the beautiful sister of a policeman. There was a cinema ad for Mystic stockings, where a kind of green witch writhed over a pair of stockings she was passing through her hands. The ad evoked this woman and hurt John. But perhaps he was familiar with being hurt; perhaps he felt at home, hurt. The few letters of his that chance has preserved suggest that hurt was an element in our acquaintanceship:

> I waited and waited on Tuesday evening and that was all. Then I thought she might be ill, or some accident, but the obvious one is almost always right, the hardest one to admit. But it doesn't matter now.

A postcard from Sligo:

> Thank you so much for the letter. It's far better to be honest. And of course it doesn't profoundly matter, anyhow.

A terse letter saying:

> What you did that last evening the more I think wasn't very far short of criminal.

(What? What did I do?)

A letter:

> The only world is the world of love, and if we're true we must be
> consumed in whatever reality there is. All the rest is silly business.

A telegram saying he waited till eight. A telegram to the Pike
Theatre wishing me luck—I was an actress, at the time, and opening that
night in a Behan one-acter. A brush-off letter:

> I think it's better for us not to meet; there's too much brokenness
> in our last evening and yesterday, a kind of inconsequence with-
> out joy, almost mere pauses or waiting, both of us coming out of
> our different lives. So let us wait apart for a while.

Then he elaborately wishes me happiness. This letter is blotched; it was
either rained on, or I cried when I read it.

Yet what I remember from the year or two we sometimes went out
together are simple things. John knew the manager of the Capitol Cinema, for instance—they were from the same part of the country. And
one day this manager stood us a meal in the restaurant, at a cosy table-
for-two at the side, up against the flock wallpaper, with our own little
lamp on the table. I can taste at this moment the rasher in that mixed grill.
It was the luxury, the lavishness of it that made it so memorable. Because
we were poor. Not intellectually—he gave me Rilke's *Notebooks of
Malte Laurids Brigge*; I introduced him to Webster, and so on. But we
walked everywhere. We had very little money. Once we went on the bus
to Skerries and relished the blowy air, out on a headland. I remember
that day because we were lighthearted and friendly, and not at our usual
edgy distance from each other. And I've seen that exact landscape, completely transformed, in one of his marvelous stories. That's one of the
pleasures of having known a writer.

I think now that Mary Lavin, who spun many a plot in her mews in
Lad Lane, promoted us to each other. There was a great deal of head-

long drama connected with knowing her. She'd send me notes saying things like—of a man we were both interested in—"he has done some bad things of which I'd like to tell you. He certainly came between us by a deviousness and secretiveness in his nature that is *not* in mine. Ah, well." And she would speed on to an instant portrait of the next person to cross her mind. She would bring her face close into my face and fix me with her gooseberry-colour eyes and enrol me in whatever the scenario of the moment was. She may have had plans for John or for me, separately or together. Underneath even her own consciousness she was frighteningly sure of what she wanted. She tunnelled towards her goals at a depth I, for one, have never been at. I hadn't read anything she wrote, at the time, so I didn't realise.

Certainly, John and I were misled by something. He was working himself out, at that time. He didn't look impressive—a slight young teacher from the country with a slow way of speaking. But his pale glance was formidable. I wrote about him to Michael, when I was telling him everything in the first flush of love. I spelt McGahern wrong. "He's the chap who is a good writer," I wrote. "This is how I classify him so you'll remember who he is—to me he's a million little things all complexed." Then I give a pen picture of him, in which I say that he is "both lonely and contemptuous." I think now that young writers toy with narratives. Maybe John toyed with certain possibilities as a way of settling himself. Certainly, we tried hard to know each other, if willing it could do it. I remember a miserable night—the last, I think—when we wandered the wintry streets for hours and still could not find any ease with each other. These things matter when you're young and have high standards. Nowadays, I bump into him once a year or so, and we just exchange friendly greetings. But I hardly know him less, in reality, than I did when we were meeting all the time.

Biographers of Irish writers will be scraping the barrel very deep if they ever come to me. But I'm representative of a certain milieu. For every real writer around, there were ten merely literary-minded people like me. Perhaps "literary Dublin" needed both kinds. It was a real place, even in the 1960s. Without question, writing mattered more than money or possessions or status in any other field. But the culture was terribly dependent on drink. There was too much public anecdotal life and not enough personal lyric life. There was too much drinking. Drinking means bad breath and crusted shirtfronts and shaking hands and bottles of milk wolfed down as a meal and waking in the morning on a pile of coats with no clean knickers and being thin, being cold, being sick. And drinking is, after all, about getting drunk. Fine people all but prostituted themselves to get the money to get stupidly drunk every single night. I saw Myles na Gopaleen urinate against the counter in Neary's one night. That's what being a drunk means: waking to the evidence of repeated lonely humiliations, that drive you further and further away from anything but drink. And whatever that kind of drinking did to men, it ruined women. I can think of only a few of the women (and I'm not one of them) who hung around McDaid's who were not, sometimes, squalid. You would think that way of life had been designed to test people to their limits. Certainly it could not be survived, only abandoned.

7

When I was first in Hull and separated from Michael, I wrote to him often. Sometime later—maybe during a row—he sent me back a packet of those letters. So I have a unique insight into the person called Nuala O'Faolain when she was twenty-one. She seems full of life, that young woman, and curious about everything around her and, though obviously madly in love, not at all abject. The only thing is, she keeps asking this man to marry her. I am astonished now to see how persistently I asked Michael to hurry up his divorce so as to marry me.

> I always hope that one day you will see what I mean by marriage [I write]. I would like to get married soon, otherwise I can't really go to live at the cottage. . . . Marrying you wouldn't be my ideal, but the ideal might well grow up between us so I wish you'd marry me, quick.

It never crossed my mind to consider marriage as an institution you could look at, walk around, detach, as a social arrangement, from particular people. I saw no connection at all between what I was planning—a husband, children—and what my mother, the woman I knew best, actually had—a husband, children. Yet her letters told a clear story:

I'm all fussed and financially desperate. Lost half-stone weight, though, and people—including Da—remark on it without it being told.

I complain about my loneliness in Hull. She replies:

I'm fat, tired, ugly, and old, and I have spent all my money and I'm not able to look after my home and my family. Contrast these truths with your easily remedied ills and brighten up.

She was still struggling with domesticity.

The rooms are a mess. I'll pay you to help me one whole day when you come home—I can't find *anything* and dirt and destruction are overwhelming me. Daddy is fine—madly cheerful, ordinary and prosperous. Marvellous at the ostrichism, about me and everything.

She has a baby.

I don't feel either well or happy, except with the baby. Money is the worst trouble—the Electricity Supply Board cut us off this morning and I have to wash filthy clothes. I wish there was some way to make him pay. The continual worry is bad for my ulcers.

She counts her blessings, unconvincingly:

Still—I have good friends, a char, the weather is fine, I have plenty of books and every so often the companionship of the older children.

I knew marriage was perilous. I had met two women who in their different ways I admired and wanted to copy. One of them was Harry Be-

wick, the artist Pauline Bewick's mother. The other was the mother of
Pauline's friend Barry: Maura Laverty, at that time one of Ireland's best-
known women writers. Neither of them had husbands.

Harry was English. She had been a married woman with two little
girls, somewhere in the north of England, when she was young. Her
husband was an alcoholic. One day, she told me, she finished reading a
book by D. H. Lawrence. That's it, she thought to herself, and put the
children in their pram and pushed it out the door, never to go back.
She'd worked—for example, as a vegetarian cook—in progressive
schools all around England and come to Ireland and lived in a cottage in
Kerry, needing very little money because she lived very simply. Then
she'd had a house in Dublin which was spoken of with awe because the
lodgers—often grown-up men—were not stopped by Harry from
sleeping with their lovers. She would have thought it was mad to do
such a thing. When I met her, she lived in an ordinary, small garden
glasshouse in a field in Wicklow. She ate frugally, and boiled water on a
little Aladdin stove, and slept when it was dark and rose when it was
light. If a mouse, say, tried to get at her muesli, she would catch the
mouse and carry it up the field and release it. If a slightly backward local
youth spied on her sunbathing, she just moved. She liked company but
she was just as contented if no one came. She read the same few books—
the writings of the Indian sage Krishnamurti—over and over again,
peering at the pages through a magnifying glass. Other than that, I
thought her way of life perfect. Yet it was the very opposite of marriage.

Maura Laverty's daughter Barry was as enviably exotic as Pauline in
the Dublin of the time. They were art students. They had wonderful
clothes: blouses copied from *Carmen Jones,* Capri pants, ballet slippers.
They had English men interested in them, not Irish boys.

Maura had written novels and did a lot of journalism and was an
expert cook and author of cookery books. And she was the sole
scriptwriter of the early television serial based on her play *Tolka Row.*
Maura was in the world of Ireland and Dublin as Harry was not. She
knew how to earn good money. She got me my first ever professional

job—passing on a commission to research authentic recipes for the new Bunratty Castle banquet. (They were only too authentic: Bunratty started off with braume brose and sew lumbarde and pety-toes in gelyce and understandably soon abandoned authenticity.) Maura lived in an elegant flat with great long windows hung with sweeps of soft muslin. But when we girls came in she would be in her bedroom. She would come out and greet us gently, and then go back into her room. She never had anything to eat with us. She never spoke about herself, much less uttered any complaint, but I used to feel loneliness coming from her. Three children were growing up on the proceeds of her hard work. Where was her husband? A husband was never mentioned. When that lovely woman died in her bed, her body was not found for days.

Yet love was supposed to work out differently for me than it had for any woman I actually knew. I went on believing that as soon as the man I loved (so far, the best candidate was Michael—because surely having orgasms meant you were in love?—but there were always other candidates) loved me equally, as soon as some magic balance had been found, history would end. We would be married and an "ideal might well grow up between us," to quote myself.

We would have been married if I'd become pregnant. Any decent man promptly married his girlfriend in those circumstances. (Then you had to think of some way to explain things, when the baby arrived, seven months into the marriage. Couples suddenly emigrated to England and Australia. Women moved across the country and gave birth and hid the babies and put pillows under their skirts when their mothers came to see them. Hundreds of babies were firmly said to be "premature.") No matter how progressive the circle you moved in, you lost almost everything if you became pregnant outside marriage. One girl in UCD did get pregnant; the others, through a combination of the most severe sanctions and idealism about marriage, kept their sexuality and their boyfriends', as far as anyone knows, in check. This girl was a distinguished person in every way. But I remember her hunched in her bedsitter in Fitzwilliam Street, a pariah; I never pass that house without thinking of her with regret. Even to say the words "expecting a baby" wasn't easy. A man I knew had to tell his mother his girlfriend was pregnant. His mother, who had been buying fruit, ran and got a big kitchen knife and plunged it into the melon in her basket. "That's what you've done to the Virgin Mary!" she cried. "That!" plunging the knife in again. "That!"

I gathered that the men I knew from down the country had lost their virginities, when they had, in the grounds of county hospitals. Nurses were often singled out as "going all the way." But it was always someone else who was having sex: nurses, actresses, Protestants in Trinity, or, from the Trinity point of view, Catholics up in UCD. Sex was in everyone's mind, often obsessively. But no one believed it was a healthy thing and good for you. Or that people who did it were altogether acceptable. In practice, in a place without contraception, the only women quite free to have sex were married women. There were so many children that it was easy to include one or two who might or might not be by the husband. Though male lovers were dangerous. They'd get maudlin and tell a whole pub about the son or daughter they had by so-and-so. At the other extreme, they forgot. I was with a friend of my father's once and he was saying to a girl in the company—this was in the early 1970s—"I don't know what you women's lib people think you're up to. Can't any woman who's worth her salt get what she wants from a man if she treats him nicely in bed?" He'd forgotten the young woman he was talking to was his own daughter from a long-ago liaison.

An old Ireland was ending, in the 1960s. There were new possibilities. But what arrangement you came to with what kind of man was still the most important question by far for a woman. And it wasn't even seen as a question. I was asking Michael to marry me as if the act of getting married made no difference to one's independence. Yet the lives around me were full of hints that there were difficulties intrinsic to being a woman, married or not. Margaret got into trouble in her Catholic home for having an ashtray with a drawing by Matisse—just one sinuous line—of a woman with a baby at the breast. Dirty, they thought it. Laila, wealthy and elegant, played French ballads on her little white portable in her room in a hotel in Harcourt Street, sprinkling Mitsouko on her cashmere jumpers, not able to sleep for fear her father in Egypt, thousands of miles away, would find out she had a boyfriend and kill her. The women in my friend Geraldine's home town in Leicestershire worked in the stocking factories. On the way to work, they left their bowls in at the fish-and-chip shop, and they collected them, full of chips and peas and faggots, at dinnertime. There was great competition among them, someone remarked to me, about the bowls. The bowls were status symbols— bowls and prams. Whoever had the biggest, most decorated bowl and pram was the most respected. You would think I would have noticed that being a wife and a mother wouldn't necessarily suit me.

Yet there I was in Hull, writing to Michael about going to a family-planning clinic to get fitted with a contraceptive device. "The bloody thing is like a medium-sized rubber pudding-bowl," I say. Then—this appals me today—I say:

> We could see what using it is like, and if you don't like it then we'll stop. I'm longing for us to have a baby and I could do it too, without inconveniencing you in any way or stopping you being free.

My mother was as unaware as I was. "I don't really care if you get a degree or not," she wrote to me, "I'd far rather see you with a husband and a few kids." This—when her burning resentment showed that she felt as trapped as a slave, kept out in a suburb with children! But she blamed the person, my father, for that. Women did blame their husbands. The idea that it was desirable for all women to go off for their lifetime with one man and have his children as their life's task was completely uncriticised. I would have blamed Michael if I had spent an unhappy life with him. But perhaps my unconscious was more alert than I was. In the same letter where I claim I can have a baby without "inconveniencing" him I recall, for no particular reason, the baby the girl I knew had had in Belfast.

I've been thinking [I write] about the motionless sadness of bringing it down from Belfast in the train. And its grandfather, playing with its fingers in the big empty church.

As for the complex of man, baby, job—it was hard to get that right, either. In my own world, men had money and interesting lives and could show you things and bring you around, whereas the radio personality Frankie Byrne, I well remember, was the only woman I personally had ever met who had bought her own house with her own earnings. There were very few women teachers in UCD. Mrs. Wall made things in history much clearer to me than Professor Dudley Edwards did, or Professor Williams. But she was a nobody in the politics of the college, compared to them. In English, Lorna Reynolds was a most generous patron, getting me proofreading work and taking me to tea (Earl Grey and lemon cake) in her lovely house. I knew she was a friend of formidable women—the novelist Kate O'Brien, for instance, and, in Italy, Darina Silone. But I also knew that in UCD she had to fight the unequal treatment accorded to single women like herself, compared to the married men who were considered the norm. "I am not responsible for your nine children, Mr. Tierney!" was the punch line of an account of one of her many brave confrontations with the then president of UCD. She was constantly embattled. And she never won.

With marriage so unconsidered a condition, no wonder there were so many bitter wives around. I remember Anthony Cronin saying once, about the 1950s, "That was the era of the spectacularly difficult wife." He was thinking of Dylan Thomas's wife, Caitlin, and William Empson's wife, Hetta. They had the problem of their husbands too, of course, as has any difficult wife I can think of. It was to be another twenty years, at least, before a wife might be perceived as herself as well as an appendage of her husband. To be a wife and hope for a career taken with the seriousness of your husband's career was hardly possible. You would have had to go to the lengths of drawing him into a defensive folie à deux, as Queenie Leavis was said to have done with F. R. Leavis in English Lit circles at Cambridge. You could best have a career—that is, express your gifts and earn your own money—by either not having sex at all or having it but somehow not getting pregnant. It happened that although I never used the device I got in the clinic and never took the pill, I didn't get pregnant.

I count that, along with being sent to boarding-school, as the crucial accident that allowed me to survive. There were other great strokes of luck, like knowing Sean Mac Réamoinn, and knowing the older man—the doctor—who kept an eye on me through college. But though I might have managed something without them, I would not have survived having a child. This has nothing to do with children as such. I love them, now. I have very deep feelings about being childless. But then I was so unskilled and so confused that I couldn't have raised a child well. Childbearing, along with bad education, relationships that managed to be simultaneously all-absorbing and unrewarding, and financial dependance—these were the enemies of promise. But that's not why I'm glad; I didn't think of myself as having promise. I'm glad because under the old system it was so easy to rear children badly. The child wouldn't have properly survived.

I didn't see that then, partly because I had no one to see it with. When the women's movement came along it was collective—its insights were shared. But before it, when "love" was all that mattered, solidarity between women was correspondingly unvalued. I certainly thought of married women as a different species from me—as women who had retired.

There was a kind of fun unmarried girls could have that married women were death to. I remember a glorious, glamorous night, just at the end of this period in my life. I'd got my big scholarship and I was about to go up to Oxford. I was twenty-three, in Rome for the first time, and burning with excitement at being there. I was with Michael and a group of theatrical people from Trinity who were putting on an evening of the actor Pat Fay in Yeats and Beckett monologues, in a crumbling old theatre near the Piazza Navona. It was a privileged way to be in the city for the first time—to belong to it by being sent out to buy needles or to stick posters to walls. Across in Vatican City, Sean Mac Réamoinn, who was at the heady opening of the second Vatican Council, might be in the bar for religious correspondents, underneath the Via della Conciliazione. Or he might be around a happy table in the garden of the trattoria in Trastevere where Irish people met. And the American I'd known in Dublin—who I had never blamed for his use of me, the night his mother died—was living in Rome. He flirted with me when no one was looking and arranged to meet me late one night in the dark hallway of the pension where Michael and I were staying. This man put me into his little car and we swooped around the wonderful city, jumping out to go into a bar; to climb up the steps of the Colosseum and sit and kiss; to walk in the still countryside, out at the Via Appia Antica, stopping to kiss; to look down on the rooftops from the Janiculum Hill, kissing; and ending in the beautiful dawn in the Campidoglio, where, beside the Renaissance square, there was a plot of grass and shrubs and a cage with two little wolf cubs stretching and playing in it. I had seen Audrey Hepburn in *Roman Holiday*. This was that, with me as the star.

This man had a wife. It meant nothing to me that he had a wife. Then, and for a long time afterwards, I was unable to bring a moral sense or even common sense to my dealing with the opposite sex—and my own sex. I think unconsciousness was the condition that allowed the culture I grew up in to exist. When change did come, about a decade later, the fog I had been wandering in was so dense that it took me ages to make my way half out of it. Which is where I am now.

8

Being with Michael was wonderfully firm ground, compared to anything else I'd known. But it was an inconclusive relationship. I discovered, after we came back from Hull and were living in Dublin while I worked for the big scholarship, that he could have started his divorce. He could have moved to marry me. But he didn't. And I had reservations, too. I still prayed and went to Mass and had crises of conscience about sleeping with him. A deeper difficulty, welling up from some bedeviling idealism, was the incoherent feeling that there was something more difficult, and therefore more right, I could do, than just live pleasantly with a decent man.

I was also imbued with the idea of "looking up" to a man. Michael was far too sceptical to accept the authority I tried to confer on him. But I hero-worshipped an intensely serious Catholic, a Welshman I had met when he visited Dublin. The possibility of marrying this Welshman and being "good" for the rest of my life was a secret ideal—and although I knew no more about being a good Catholic bourgeois wife than the man in the moon, I was perfectly sincere. I knew him for years, we wrote scores of letters to each other, and he did in the end—out of niceness, when I was upset about something else—propose to me. When I said yes, he immediately disappeared. It turned out he'd gone to see his mother. Then he came back to me and asked to call our arrangement off. He smelled the dance halls off me, whether he knew it or not. I never saw him again, but I heard that he entered the priesthood, and eventually left it, and married and had a large family.

He did change my life, however, by asking me, when he was an undergraduate, to visit him at Oxford. I saw the little city for the first time, silent, after heavy snow, in the depth of winter. It was magical. Yet it wasn't magic; a person could go there. When I won the big scholarship a few years later, that was where I chose to go.

Even before I was there with the Welshman, I'd had a dream of Oxford. I had read a book about it one day, on my father's boat. This was a temporary folly of his. He kept it at the slipway at Clontarf Yacht Club, where his own grandfather and grandmother had been steward and housekeeper to the toffs. We puttered across to the mouth of the Liffey, once or twice, and left my father off at the water steps at Butt Bridge, beside the *Evening Press*. Going to work by boat made us one with all the dead people who had used Dublin Bay. Sometimes we went the other way—the boat plunging and bucking—around past the Baily lighthouse to Howth. It was on one of those journeys, with the spray breaking over me, that I finished reading *Dusty Answer* by Rosamund Lehmann. If the boat had sunk I would have gone on reading till I was under the waves. It had college friends in England in it, and it was the novel that formed my idea of college undergraduate life. I thrilled to all the great romantic books. My friend's mother threw a teapot at me during *A Farewell to Arms* and I didn't miss a sentence. Scott Fitzgerald made me tremble with empathy. My mother quoted bits of *Ballad of the Sad Café* to me. But it was English people in books—even as far back as *The Chalet School* stories and Angela Brazil—who summed up glamour. *The Constant Nymph* fed this fantasy, and *The Green Hat*, and a Daphne du Maurier novelette on a faintly incestuous theme, which quoted the refrain of Edna St. Vincent Millay:

We were very tired,
We were very merry,
We had gone back and forth
All night on the ferry.

I yearned after the troubled, rich, English upper-class people in books like that.

In real life, glamour consisted of my friend and myself getting done up in high heels and tight black skirts. Tucked into the skirts, and anchored by wide elastic belts, we wore men's white nylon shirts with the sleeves rolled up. We had big pointy breasts (old nylons stuffed in our bras), a thick layer of yellowy Pan-Stik on our faces, black lines going up from the corners of our eyes, Vaseline on our shocking-pink lips. In the Crystal Ballroom we two beauties eyed guys with duck's-arse haircuts and crepe-soled shoes, while we condescended to dance with awestruck Malaysian students.

I was wrong about *Dusty Answer*. The story turns out to involve Cambridge, not Oxford. And in the mid-1960s, when I went there, the generality of Oxford students were not glamorous. The *Brideshead Revisited* style was in temporary retreat. The Beatles had just burst upon England and were about to change it and the world. But I couldn't have been happier when I scuffed through the leaves to the college that had accepted me, one day in the autumn of 1963. I always knew underneath how near I had been to a lifetime of some clock-watching, achingly pointless job. When I was seventeen, I'd worked for a while in the canteen of a water-softener factory near Heathrow airport. That kind of job. Now here I was, in one of the first minidresses, with nothing to do but study, and a partner on the side. Michael was going to teach in Italy while I was doing this degree, but we would meet in the vacations. My friend Harden Rodgers started at Cambridge the same year. When the girl beside her at dinner the first night asked her where she was from, and Harden said "Ireland," the girl said, "Oh—you'll be wanting the praties, then." I never thought of being from Ireland. I belonged. I had read so many novels about this. That was where I came from—from inside the books I'd read.

Oxford was an unpretentious place, then. It was a provincial English town, which happened to have the beautiful buildings of an old university tucked away in it. The centre was decayed and ordinary. There were enclaves of small houses where working people lived and had prams and net curtains, behind and between the buildings of the colleges. There were brown varnished pubs where locals with Oxfordshire accents played bar billiards. There were corner shops, not wine bars and boutiques. There was an old-fashioned department store, with a tearoom where you could get anchovy toast. It is a discount place now, featuring Evans Outsizes. There were ancient, crooked coaching inns: only their names—the Mitre, the Golden Cross—live on in the shopping arcades full of souvenir shops that stand where they stood. There were proper cafés. I saw Auden trying to eat a poached egg in the Cadena, after a night presumably—by the shake in his hands—as miserable as his little basalt eyes. Nowadays, Oxford is full of tourists all the time. Then it was sometimes so empty that its wonderful weathers filled it. In the sluggish summers, the foaming green countryside around seemed to press on it. Then cold seeped up from the flooded river, and fog rolled along the pitted golden walls of the colleges, and rainwater rustled down the gullies beside the footpaths. I once passed Elizabeth Taylor—in Oxford to stand there as Helen of Troy in Richard Burton's production of *Doctor Faustus*—hurrying along a back lane just as the winter night fell. Her violet eyes when she glanced up were so intense, so exotic, that they seemed to fix like a flashbulb a permanent impression of the flint and wet cobble and black stone of winter Oxford.

I borrowed—this is an important period detail—a leather jacket and auditioned before the board of the Oxford University Dramatic Society to direct their annual play in the Playhouse Theatre. This was a very prestigious thing to do, and that I was chosen to do it is a sign of how much change there was in the 1960s. No woman had directed the OUDS play for forty years. Not that I rose to the call of social change very well;

my production of *The Importance of Being Earnest* was mediocre, except for Maria Aitken, and the set was terrible. The London newspapers traditionally reviewed the OUDS play, so this did not go unnoticed. One of them said it looked as if it were happening in a bed-sitter in Golders Green.

But leather jackets and young Irishwomen directors were all part of the new style. When I met people who had been up at Oxford only ten years earlier they remembered greyness and conservatism. But the 1960s were bright. There was a feeling of youthful licence. I remember a particularly abandoned party in Christ Church where the boys from the group The Animals were actually among the revellers. (Most of the time it was just young Oxford men trying to look as if they were The Animals.) I was living my usual divided life. For the first year or so, I was a practising Catholic; in the ugly church in St. Giles, one Good Friday, the liturgy was in English for the first time in my life. We, the congregation, had to say, "Crucify Him! Crucify Him!" I was very shaken by this. I went to the decorous events of the Newman Society, where young Catholics were meant to meet Catholics of the opposite sex. But I dropped that as my social life got busier and busier.

I see now that being Irish was quite fashionable in that brief period between the 1960s discovery of the working class and the Northern Ireland troubles starting. I see that those years were a little space in history when young women were free and freely available but hadn't yet woken to the implications of freedom. To think, I debated something about women with the scholar Dame Helen Gardner for the amusement of the hearties of a private dining club. The fellows actually lolled around in evening dress and swigged champagne by the neck as we women sparred to amuse them! And we didn't see it! Class lines in England were not really under attack in the 1960s. You only had to look at these men to see they could never consider themselves anything but lords of the universe. And gender issues were deeply buried. I went to see Tintern Abbey, on the Welsh border, with an American suitor of mine. I had a room of my own in the hotel, but I knew it was understood that a bed might be shared. But when he came to my room he found the door locked. This—with no explanation—offended him dreadfully, and we went back to Oxford in silence. But I couldn't say—I literally could not find any way of saying—that my period had unexpectedly started. I could have slept with him, but I couldn't say those words. I imagine that countless such misunderstandings happened, before the women's revolution took some of the power out of that kind of taboo. When I hear the Beatles' "I Wanna Hold Your Hand," its slight plangency, more than anything, brings back the feel of those years. We were only young. There was something pitiable about our playing with freedom.

The poet W. R. Rodgers came to Oxford for a day. Bertie was my friend Harden's father, and at her request he took me around with him. He was a wild drinker. We racketed up and down Oxford in taxis; we even went to part of a lecture by Isaiah Berlin, on Herder. Bertie fell off the bench in the lecture hall in St. Catherine's. Enid Starkie gave us drinks. She wrote me a note afterwards that catches the flavour of the day:

> Dear Miss O'Faolain,
>
> I hope your uncle got back safely. I hope that you did not think me too unhospitable. If you are out of pocket for the taxi, will you allow me to pay for it? 1) I would have taken your uncle home if I had not been busy and 2) I have much more money than you have! Your uncle mentioned something about a cheque he had hoped the Davins would cash for him.

Acquaintances mistaken for uncles. Questionable cheques. It was that kind of day. But Bertie did me a very great favour when he introduced me to what, by the end of the evening, were his somewhat tight-lipped hosts, Dan and Winnie Davin. Their house was to be a second home—a first home, in many ways—to me. They were New Zealanders, and Dan had been a Rhodes Scholar and then a distinguished wartime officer and historian and novelist, and was now a fellow of Balliol and ran the Oxford University Press. I soon had a little attic room in their hospitable book-stuffed house. In a recent biography of Dan, he and I are supposed to have been in love, but really we were that much more comfortable thing, a mutual admiration society.

I learnt, just from knowing Dan and Winnie and the people they knew. That's one of the great things about university towns. Picking up an education was a dimension of social life. The Davins had a corner they drank in in their local pub, and anyone might come along. Godfrey Lienhardt was an anthropologist, specialising in the Dinka of the southern Sudan, but a great generalist, too, and a most cultivated man. He was there most nights. People talked about books, and when this or that book passed my way, I read it. Kierkegaard. Fontane. Benjamin Constant. Christina Stead. I met people. Iris Murdoch made it quite clear that just because she was born in Blessington Street didn't mean she was Irish. An American translator of the *Iliad* talked about Scott-Moncrieff and how he'd picked the wrong line from Shakespeare to represent *A la Recherche du Temps Perdu* in the title of his translation of Proust. "Remembrance of things past" was too soft, this man said. It didn't catch the hard stroke of *recherche*. The imperative tone of "Tell me where all past things are" would be more faithful to Proust's rhythm. John Wain, who was a man of letters as well as a popular novelist, talked about Doctor Johnson and taught me to play shove ha'penny. Richard Ellman, the great biographer of James Joyce, came in. The great biographer of George Eliot, Gordon Haight, came in. He was typical of the grandees of the American Wasp academic establishment, who would arrive in Oxford in the course of research visits they conducted like royal progresses. They stayed at rich, discreet hotels and took people to dinner at their London clubs. If they were the definitive scholars in their field they were usually published by the OUP, so they came to see the Davins.

My thesis on "The Reception of George Moore's *Esther Waters*" was about a kind of crossroads in late-nineteenth-century history of ideas and was full of interest. By definition, once I did any work at all on it, I knew more about the subject than anyone else. But there were also set papers in the B. Phil. exam, and I knew hardly anything about that subject matter. I cycled off from time to time to read a perfunctory essay to this old man in a study here or this old lady in a set of rooms there— obscure dons who had somehow ended up with responsibility for Matthew Arnold or Kipling or Gissing or whoever. The university didn't teach at this level; if you didn't seek out learning for yourself, it would not be put your way. I wasn't learning.

I was saved, however, by the labour historian Raphael Samuel. As if he were the angel of his name, he came to me, even though I hardly knew him, and presented me with a cake in a tin that his mother had sent him and told me firmly that he would help me to work. He gave me essays to do every week—"The growth of a reading public," "Chartist oratory," "The novels of 'Mark Rutherford.'" He took me to a study group in Nuffield where people talked about Paley and Defoe and Spengler and the Bryant and May strike and Dostoevsky and Henry Mayhew and Trotsky and Peterloo. Raphael was a pioneer of the interdisciplinary approach. He believed that anyone who had done a specialist degree had been trained in incuriosity about everything else. He believed in starting again, from ignorance. I was rich in ignorance. I count it as one of the great lucky things in my life—besides going to boarding-school and not getting pregnant, and then Michael being married and having Sean Mac Réamoinn as a friend—that Raphael took me in hand.

It was far more important than it seemed, even at the time, to be introduced to labour history. It fed into the social revolutions that were just about to come. One side effect was that the physical world of England began to be meaningful to me. I would know enough to understand why a canal had been cut in a certain place, or what the name of a pub probably referred to, or around what time the words FRIENDLY SOCIETY had probably been painted on an old office window. A similar infusion of meaning into the landscapes and townscapes of France came through Richard Cobb, when I got to know him—a scholar who used things like Simenon's novels or the route of the Tour de France as means towards understanding French society.

But I learnt most from the man I fell in love with, halfway through my time at Oxford. From the moment I met him I enrolled in his one-person university. He conducted it in pubs, walking the streets, in wonderful letters packed and bursting with knowledge and ideas. He knew about the history of art and about paintings, which were his great passion. But he also knew about model villages, how to play bar billiards, classic French cooking, the early history of Aston Villa, Soviet songs, the history of witchcraft. . . . He was loud and happy and shabby and vivid, and—impersonal. He and I didn't talk about personal things. Sometimes his almost hectic bonhomie seemed to still, when I caught his real attention. It was a challenge to get him to attend to the personal.

He was just leaving Oxford, and I had a year to go. We had absolutely no money. We squatted in a basement and he bought books on account in one bookshop and sold them immediately in a secondhand bookshop to get us cash to drink and eat a bit. It was summer. I happen to have a piece of paper we must have doodled on during some long day talking in a pub. He has drawn a map of England. I've written in the few places whose location I happened to know: London, Liverpool, Crewe, Hull. He has filled in the names of the rest. If we had both been English, things would have been different. But we weren't. However, in 1966 it didn't matter.

I'll call the ghost who looks like this young man "Rob." In 1997 I was invited to speak about Ireland at a conference of politicians and bankers and diplomats, in Oxford. The organisers put me up in the Randolph Hotel, in the centre of town. I looked down on the stretch of street I had walked along, when I came to visit the Welshman, in the depths of winter, long ago. We had come up from the station, my hand in his in the warmth of the pocket of his duffle coat, up Beaumont Street, across into the Broad, past the sculptured heads outside the Sheldonian and the domes of the Sheldonian Theatre and the Radcliffe Camera, all covered in frost, all shimmering in the moonlight. Silent and shining, as I was never to see the place again. The streetscape was no less fine as I looked at it more than thirty years later. But it meant nothing more than itself.

A street away was the spot where I had my first rendezvous with Rob. I needed to work on what I would say at the conference. But his ghost was in my way. Cold rain was spilling down that morning, but I walked out from the hotel to the field beside the Thames called Port Meadow. That night—the night of the day I met him—had been warm and close. We'd lain on the grass on the bank of the river—here? No, further on. The fishermen had made clinking noises, very quietly, across the sleek river, under the black hedge. Then we needed more privacy and we went back across the meadow and down into the soft high weeds on the bank of the canal. I followed that path again. That must have been the spot, I said to myself, standing above the canal, shivering. There. I was wet and cold and bored, that morning. But I was trying to get rid of stubborn memory—to mock it, to force it out to the dim distance it should inhabit.

One swirling, shadowy image somehow sums that time up. It isn't of me or Rob. It was something I saw for a minute, late one winter night, in Paddington Station. I'd been in London with Rob, and now I was going back up to Oxford on the last train. The big caverns of the station were dark and full of gusts of wind. A man I knew by sight was talking desperately to a woman, beside the train. He was very beautiful and she—I saw it was his young wife—was beautiful, too. He had his hands in her long hair and he was crying. She was crying, too. She had a white coat on. They kept kissing each other desperately. That romantic sadness is what I was expecting of Oxford, from *Dusty Answer*. But I'm not sure whether that's what I really experienced, in that part of my life, or whether I imposed it, from my imagination. And if so, whether I imposed it then or afterwards, gradually.

All I know is that when I left Oxford and went back to Dublin, I faced into the future looking backwards. I was half a girl still. I was half heartbroken. The place I was leaving had from beginning to end contained feelings so vehement, however silly they were, that even now it is hard to believe they don't live, still, somewhere else as well as in my memory. I looked down at the paving stones as I hurried back to the hotel through the rain, that wet morning in 1997, and I interrogated the pavement, half as a joke. "You're made of fine big slabs of granite," I said to it. "Are you the same stones I walked on then? And, if so, why are you not crying out?"

9

When I came back to Dublin from Oxford, the English Department in University College Dublin was more ticking over than being run. I got a job there. Not many years later, when the burst of prosperity that opened things up in the mid-1960s was spent, I would have had to have a publications record. As it was, I was soon commissioned to edit an anthology of Beckett criticism. This came about through being taken up by a very well-known English academic who came to Dublin to give a lecture. I lived high up above Merrion Square, in an old flat where the servants had once lived, underneath the roof. He came back there, after an increasingly breathless day wandering Dublin, but left dramatically because my bedspread was the same as the one on his son's bed at home. He sent a card from the airport: "The end of a sensing," it said, referring with a certain wit to the title of a recent book by the critic Frank Kermode, *The Sense of an Ending*. This man arranged the Beckett commission.

He was one of three or four established academics who took an interest in me in those years. That was how it was, and perhaps is, when you are a young woman in a male-dominated field. The men dispensed patronage. They would tell you where the jobs were and get you invited to conferences and endorse you for grants and mention your name to publishers. This wasn't exactly corrupt but it wasn't fair, either; they wouldn't do it for you if they didn't like you or if they didn't feel you were personally grateful. I didn't see any general truths such as that, of course. I was blinded by the habit of translating everything into personal terms. I saw the academic world around me as being comprised of such-and-such a nice man and such-and-such a nasty man, and so on; I didn't notice that it was ninety-nine percent comprised of men. I didn't ask any of them for help. I wanted to be liked, not helped. I had no sense of being at the start of a career. My aim in life was something to do with lov-· ing and being loved. That was going to work out, somehow. In the meantime, and on the side, I did the job of lecturing to huge classes of students on texts which, in UCD in the mid-1960s, no one had ever considered in the light of whether they might interest students.

Pater—I remember talking about Walter Pater in a lecture theatre so long and narrow that in the rows at the back the boys were reading newspapers—studying the racing pages with a view to a bet, no doubt—and even smoking, while the nuns at the front wrote down everything I said. I remember giving imploring lectures on Newman. A lot of the students had just come out of Catholic schools and pretended to be pious. If you asked them, they picked something like "The Hound of Heaven" as their favourite poem, in case the boss class still wanted that of them. But most of them didn't want to make the serious forays into the moral life that the writers we were teaching asked of them: Shakespeare, Milton, Wordsworth, Newman. I was lecturing on "The Idea of a University" in 1968 when the students came up with a few of their own ideas about a university. I knew about the anti-Vietnam protests in the USA and the *évènements* in Paris, but I couldn't have been more astonished at an authentic protest happening in UCD.

The student revolution was nothing much in itself, as might be guessed from the fact that its heroes call it the "gentle" revolution. The main hall at UCD became very untidy, because, with the students sitting in, it could not be swept. At least one meeting of the Academic Council was blockaded, and the worthies couldn't get to the toilets. Unpleasant mimeographed estimates of the teaching staff's capabilities were circulated—at least the one about me was unpleasant. "Miss O'Faolain is so authoritarian and sarcastic that many leave her tutorials and will not approach the Department office while she is there"; that's what *Confrontation*, the pamphlet of the Students for Democratic Action, said. I deserved it; I did use sarcasm as a weapon to try to smash the students' blandness. And I did believe in laying down the law. But my personality wasn't the problem. The problem was that the college had fallen into decay. The staff/student ratio in the English department was 1 to 250. Students had to make an appointment to talk to someone on the academic staff, and they might have to wait two weeks. Examination formats were changed without consultation. And things were even worse in other areas, like architecture. The institution was so inert that no one in authority had perceived that a revolt was inevitable. You could see confusion and even fear in the faces of the older academics, so accustomed were they to docility.

I was a contented product of the old system. And I was too young myself to respect students so young. They were right to complain that they had no more input into the way things were done than they'd had at secondary school. But they weren't very different, themselves, to my eyes, from secondary school pupils. I had a messianic belief in the capacity of the academic study of English literature to change a person utterly. But all but a few of the students thought "doing English" was grinding out essays on the three stages of Wordsworth's relationship with nature or the role of the Fool in King Lear. I knew myself that "doing English" was easy on one level. But I wanted my students to do something hard, to learn to hold on to the self while going out of the self to enter into the literature that someone else had made—to find a poise between subjectivity and objectivity. This poise would then be rehearsed and made more stable with each access of understanding of a piece of art. The change in the person comes in that; it isn't a matter of learning a technical vocabulary. There is a vocabulary peculiar to the study of literature, literature itself never having asked to be studied. A university

English department—a place where the autonomy of a piece of literature is subsumed to the supposedly civilising purpose of the academy—uses that vocabulary. And some smart students picked up this special vocabulary by reading the critics for whom it was really expressive, and they parroted it so well that they thought they understood. But not many of them did understand. They weren't changed in themselves.

The night students—teachers and policemen and civil servants coming into Earlsfort Terrace on dark winter nights—shivering in their damp coats, grimly addressing themselves to a most unfriendly syllabus, hardly ever understood. But I admired those people. In fact, I half loved them. When I lectured at night I used to end the hour as exhausted as a performer, from the effort of trying to show the texts properly to such serious people. The night students were, metaphorically speaking, the proletariat of the student revolution. They hadn't time to revolt. They were only interested in getting what they could from the system. The day students were the middle classes; they had the leisure and the self-confidence to force change on the authorities.

The professionalising of the college began around then. Before that, it was something of a friendly shambles. The ladies in the front office made a great many bureaucratic decisions. The head porter, Paddy Keogh, ran the teaching operation. If a lecturer with a drink problem rang up from a pub down the street to say—as one did when I was with him—that he was in Bray and cut off by floods, Paddy would rearrange the lecture or find someone else to give it. Professors were such for life. So if someone like the historian Desmond Williams, for instance, found himself uninterested in most aspects of being a university teacher from very early in his career, no comment was attracted. If Desmond disappeared in mid-lecture-series it wouldn't have occurred to anyone to protest. In fact, probably only Paddy Keogh would have known.

On the other hand, the teachers—Desmond among them—were still people you could talk and drink all day with, or go to the afternoon pictures with, or borrow money from, or lend money to. The peer group wasn't defined by status. It was made up of different kinds of people who had in common that they drifted around the St. Stephen's Green area, trading short-term pleasure for long-term strain and difficulty. I might set out in the morning to do a bit of work but end up drinking whiskey with historians in the Arts Club, or at a Eucharist (brown bread and off-licence Beaujolais; we'd finish the bottle afterwards) organised by Sean Mac Réamoinn in someone's flat; or maybe I'd have bumped into the poet John Montague coming out of a gloomy building in derelict Temple Bar and drift on with him to the little house in Ballsbridge, its tables covered with bottles of pills, the poet John Berryman was living in. I might have burrowed into a company that had settled down in Hartigan's or O'Dwyer's by four in the afternoon. I might head for the National Library and never get closer than Buswell's. Someone might have won money on a horse. Paddy Kavanagh might beckon from a doorway to run to the chemist for him. A lot of people lived in an uncommitted public way. If they had home lives somewhere, they were hardly mentioned. I sometimes went back to Merrion Square to bed with an acquaintance in the afternoons, before he went home to his family. He was almost the only man I knew who, if he had any responsibilities to wife and children, attempted to discharge them.

I think a lot of the people around lacked, like me, the kind of inner balance that young people seem to have now. There had always been a censored literature in Ireland; now, books that truly appalled, like *Last Exit to Brooklyn*, were handed around. There had been an unbroken silence about sexuality; now, films like Ingmar Bergman's presented the erotic to Irish people, whom it made shy. The world darkened; the ambulance brigade people stood at the back of the cinema to help anyone in the audience who fainted at the realism of the nuclear horror in *The War Game*. The first drugs other than alcohol were coming in, to a generation who had been treated like infants by de Valera and Archbishop John Charles McQuaid. I went to Morocco with a gay man friend, and we were not able to be anything but madly reckless. The young boys we were with could only either murder us or protect us. We went—stoned—to *Hamlet*, done in classical Arabic, but left it to go back to eat more hash, because we thought we had been at the play for four or five hours. A predatory Italian sailor took us to a disco among pine trees, where in a divided cage a mangy lion crouched on one side of the partition and a moth-eaten tiger on the other. Frank Sinatra sang "Strangers in the Night" over and over in the hot dark. The animals smelled as if they were rotting. We obeyed dodgy characters when they told us to follow them to empty hotels with cracked swimming pools. We abandoned each other for a while. My friend came back with his face bruised. I was sick. In Dublin, he went back to his respectable job; I put on my academic gown and went back to lecturing. The biggest difference among the people who moved around the centre of Dublin was between those who knew something about self-preservation and those who knew nothing.

I am still acquainted with a lot of the people I knew in Dublin around 1970. But most of them are so different now that the past might never have been. I remember the vulnerable, not always dignified young people who are, now, dignitaries: a judge, a professor, a feared critic, a consultant. In a more confident culture, people like these would claim their youth. In North America, people, however powerful they become, are happy to go to reunions to recapture the innocence of youth. But I think middle-aged Irish people feel that they are much more innocent now than they were then.

And middle-aged members of the Irish establishment behave as if there is no history between them. There is a pretence that no feelings are in play between people who have been acquainted with each other for decades. I thought about this a few years ago when I was presenting *Booklines* on RTÉ television and the *Field Day Anthology of Irish Literature* came out. Professor Seamus Deane, its general editor, was going to come on the programme to talk about it—to say something, too, about why the modern history of women wasn't part of its account of the history of the island. I often interviewed people I had known. Each of these people came with this flavour or that. The flavour of Seamus Deane was one of the most complex. He was a colleague of mine when I was teaching in UCD, and a most brilliant one. I conducted a postgraduate seminar on Yeats's "Among Schoolchildren" with him once. I remember the room exactly and the light in it and the faces of the students, and how that great poem seemed to give up its riches. I'd count that among the most exciting couple of hours of my life.

Seamus was a hero to me when we were young teachers. He was a sensationally interesting literary critic, but above all he was the first Northerner from a nationalist background I had ever known. What he said about how his family in the Bogside ghetto in Derry was treated under the Stormont and B-Special régime was like something out of a frightening book. He was a very modern man, in some ways. He had just come back from Berkeley, and the house he lived in with Marian and the children was itself like a piece of California. A new friend, an American writer and critic called Leslie Fiedler, went out there with me a couple of times, and the four of us lolled around in the open-plan room with the picture window and drank champagne and were lighthearted. But Northern Ireland was where Seamus really stood. He had a complex contempt for Dublin. He was watching the people around him closely and judging them. It was as if they were summing up "the South" to him. He would say of someone he didn't like that they had "no speed, no style, no silence," and he'd say about people he admired, like the writers Tom Kilroy and Tom Kinsella, that they were "whole." I was proud to have the position of confidante. He advised me:

> You don't belong in hysteria, wild mobilities, pub drives (never crawls), promiscuities, endless charities with yourself as donation.

That was when we were colleagues. Then I left Dublin, and I didn't see Seamus again till a James Joyce conference in Paris a few years later. He barely spoke to me. Leslie Fiedler and his wife looked at me as

Seamus innocently waved at us in a café and walked past to join others. "Well, our lives have moved on," I said, and that was of course all that had happened. "We don't even live in the same country," I said.

So there was that little personal history somewhere in my consciousness when we met in the television studio for *Booklines*. I'd spent the days since I got the anthology studying it. It was a very grand undertaking. We'd been waiting for it for years. It was Seamus's biggest public act: a massive effort at national self-description. But something had happened between women and men in the interval between Seamus's and my youth and the publication of the anthology. The women's movement had happened. Women had emerged from the silence of the past and had begun to make their marks. I could not find in myself, talking to Seamus about the book, an unemotional response to its omission of women's testimony. The anthology was a history, of course, not a mere collection of literary texts; that's why I expected the momentous change in the condition of women in twentieth-century Ireland to be there. But I wasn't sure myself whether the tiny raw spot left from Paris was not a part of what was almost grief at the absence of women. As if not acknowledging me in the café had been writ large.

The *Field Day* is a wonderful anthology for much of its great length, and we talked about its successes for most of the time we had. Then I brought up the missing women. He said words to the effect that he really hadn't noticed what he was doing. He just hadn't noticed. This helpless tone was entirely accurate, I felt. He was weary and baffled and he didn't want an argument. I overheard Seamus Heaney saying, not long afterwards, "Why doesn't Seamus Deane defend himself? There's a perfectly good case to be made for the anthology the way it is." But Seamus Deane let it go, whether from ennui or shame it was up to the world to guess.

When we had finished the interview that day, and we were getting up from our chairs and disentangling microphone cables and saying our thanks, he paused beside me and said, "I'm sorry I hurt you." Did he mean back then or now? Did he mean "you" as in me, or "you" as in women? And *was* he sorry? The remark was masterly; it restored the preponderance of power to him, after a brief dip in my favour, when I had turned to the woman question in the interview.

This is an example of the histories that inform the ostensibly purely civic life of a place. They complicate Ireland enormously—North/ South, man/woman, then/now. Seamus had a house near mine before he went back to America. A few years ago I was walking up his road when a squad car bustled past, *ee-aw, ee-aw*. Ahead of me I saw Seamus come out and peer up the road after the back of the squad car, the way people do. Then he walked down to his gate and out to his car and went comfortably around it, his hands in his pockets, kicking a tire or two. I held back a bit, till he went in. There's not the slightest problem about saying a friendly "hello." But the "hello," for me anyway, is one of the many in this town and this country that slightly reverberates.

There was a James Joyce conference in Dublin in 1968, and all of us in the UCD English Department were involved. That's where I met Leslie Fiedler. My friend Sean Mac Réamoinn happened to be sitting on the next bar stool to him in the Lincoln Tavern.

Leslie was famous in America at the time for pioneering populist critical works with great titles—*Love and Death in the American Novel* was one; an essay on homosexual feeling in *Huckleberry Finn* called "Come Back to the Raft Ag'in, Huck Honey!" was another. Leslie was a novelist, too, and a traveller, and he loved food and drink and people. Over the next few years he showed me things like the Jewish side to Joyce's places: the grave in Trieste where Stanislaus Joyce was unobtrusively buried, sidelined as usual, and the little stones that had been left on it by mourners of his wife, who was Jewish. The purification baths and kosher cafés off the Place des Vosges in Paris. The synagogue in Rome. Leslie came and rescued me when all my money was stolen in Venice. I went and rescued him at a party in New York, when a beautiful girl who had been hitting Norman Mailer in the face was getting ready to hit him, too. He looked like Neptune, and he was a proper Jewish patriarch in his personal life. He was also a great connoisseur of popular culture. We went in and out of the singles bars one night along Second Avenue, to see how quickly we—separately—would be picked up. (Very fast. Both of us.) We went to the movie *Beyond the Valley of the Dolls*, and it gave him days of pleasure. I made some kind of contribution with him to a supposedly authoritative seminar on Joyce in 1970, in a palazzo in Trieste. I remember standing on the podium singing "Put another nickel in,/ See Our Lady in her skin,/ All I want is loving you/ and music, music, music." This school playground ditty was central to some new reading in *Ulysses* we had thought up in a bar.

We were silenced, once. The film director John Huston was interested in making a film based on *The Tempest*, and he wanted to talk to Leslie about a script. Huston was at his house in East Galway. Leslie asked whether he could bring me with him, and we headed off on the train to stay a weekend.

Huston's house was a simple, perfect Georgian manor in a wide landscape of big fields and stone walls. He lived there because it is hunting country. The driveway crossed a stream beside which hawks were caged—I saw a walk-in fridge later, stuffed with the chilled day-old chicks the hawks were fed on. Lovely horses grazed in paddocks across from the hall door, which opened into a beautifully proportioned hall room, full of precious things; I understood Huston had contacts at Shannon Airport who greatly assisted his antique collecting. Some of the staff led us to our rooms. I had a luxurious suite, with the most wonderful bedside things: There were new books and magazines and flowers and a calligraphed card with the house phone numbers of the household staff, and also a little medical kit that included a selection of sleeping tablets. Everything was perfect. The master of the house himself was found in a pitch-dark room, peering at a small television. It was a great moment. *Apollo 11* was just at that moment landing on the moon. We watched the juddering grey-and-white images, as Armstrong stepped onto that unimaginable surface. Huston was a reserved man, and Leslie hid his serious feelings under an impenetrable geniality. But this was a very great moment for America. I stayed quiet behind them. I think they were both very moved.

Later, we moved into a sitting room and the two of them chatted, sizing each other up. Huston said a very interesting thing about Marilyn Monroe, when he was directing her in *The Misfits*. She thought she would keep her looks if only she got enough sleep, he said. So she took a lot of sleeping tablets, and while she was half sedated by them, Paula Strasberg would read her lines to her, over and over. The next day, Marilyn would take barbiturates to counteract the sleeping tablets and finally arrive on the set. And she would know her lines. She'd know the main words in them and how long they were. She would know the exact rhythm of each line. But she would get the tenses all wrong. She wouldn't know whether a given line was in the past tense or the future tense or the present. I have often brooded on that.

I knew nothing about class and America then. If I had, I might have noticed how Jewish Leslie seemed in that ambiance, and how Wasp Huston seemed. Leslie was a nervy, sensitive, rubicund little man from Newark, New Jersey. He didn't suit being taken to lean on a fence by Huston in impeccable tweeds, to discuss the hunters in the field. But we might have stuck it out except for the meals. These—lunch as well as dinner—were formal occasions, served in the dining room where the wallpaper was handmade eighteenth-century Chinese, or something of the kind. Various silent children, done up like the children of the English aristocracy in white knee socks and velvet headbands, sat at the table, their meal administered either by a nanny or, in the case of one exquisite little boy, by his equally exquisite mother. She appeared to be a Bolivian from Rome and to be living out the back, where a stable yard had been converted to residences. Presumably, she was a mistress of Huston's and the child was his, and so were all the other children. He didn't say. He said little or nothing at those glacial meals. Leslie, the soul of happy appetite in normal circumstances, withered under the silence. We had dinner the first night, lunch the second day. Then we made a furtive plan around the side of the house, under a window, where no one could see us. Leslie proffered some excuse, and we were driven to the railway halt where the train back to Dublin would pause. We were hours too early. Mind? We didn't mind. The Huston car disappeared and we were left at the little station, just us, in the miles and miles of summery countryside. We jigged up and down the platform shouting and laughing, in transports of relief at getting away from the tension of that household and Huston's coldness.

My long friendship with Michael had faded away. The important times were when I went to England to see Rob. He took me to the town in Lancashire his family came from. He was such a well of historical knowledge, and had such an eye for the way a place had been made and the distinctive things in it, that travelling around with him was a revelation. Sometimes he came over to Dublin on the boat. It came into Dun Laoghaire early in the morning. I'd still be asleep when the bell from the front door jangled in my attic in Merrion Square. I'd stumble to the window in my nightdress. There, four storeys below on the empty footpath, in the clean morning where nothing moved but the seagulls, would be his upturned face. I'd throw down the keys and jump back into bed and in a minute hear his footsteps coming running up the stairs. I remember those exultant mornings when I pass that corner.

But we fought, too. I was jealous. He was jealous. We didn't know each other's lives. One Christmas he was in London and I was in Dublin. But someone thought he was in Dublin. I came into the hallway of the house one day and took the post out of my box and ripped open the cards as I went up the stairs. I didn't notice that one letter was addressed to him and had been sent on. *Dearest Rob*, I read before I knew what I was doing, *I have lost our baby*. Who this woman was and what had been happening I never grasped. The huge blaze of jealousy and grief that consumed me—I had never managed to get pregnant by him—wiped everything out. I could walk through the wintry mornings to Earlsfort Terrace to teach; I could manage nothing else. I had rung with shaking hands the hospital in London she'd written from, to try to find out her full name. A suspicious nurse had hung up on me.

In endless urgent phone calls from London he said nonsense; it was nothing, all a mistake, the girl was a fantasist, I was the only one, see—really I was—we would get married. He would get a special licence. He hurried everything up. He got the licence. We were booked into St. Pancras registry office and a few friends would join us in Yates's Wine Lodge down the road for wedding drinks. He was lent an old mill house in Somerset for the honeymoon. The time of the registry office was such-and-such. The time of the train, change at Bristol, was such-and-such, and it would connect with the bus. A neighbour would have the house in the country warmed. Bustle bustle. Forget the letter.

So one February night I was in the attic in Merrion Square doing last-minute things so I could go to London in a few days and get married. I was making a list, beside the fire, crouched right in beside the bright wig-wam of briquettes. I could hear the gusty wind and the rain it spattered on the slates just over my head. The bell from the front door went. I peered down from the window, and below, where the traffic swished by in the rain, I could see a big car idling and the man who had got out of it standing on the doorstep. I ran down the stairs and hauled the front door open.

"Daughter!" my father greeted me. "Get your coat! We're going to play dominoes in Ringsend." He thrust a big bouquet of flowers into my hands and backed away. He had never called to Merrion Square in the two years I'd been living there. He was on duty; the dominoes would be part of his "Dubliner's Diary" column the next day. I sometimes bumped into him around town, but I didn't go places with him. "I can't, Da," I began. "I'm up to my eyes—" Then I realized that it wasn't rain on his face. He was crying.

We went off in the car, and he made steady small-talk for the hour or so we were together—except once, when he said over his shoulder, waiting to get served at the bar in the crowded pub, "Don't marry him. You'll only have all the trouble of getting divorced." "Well," I said. That was the longest private conversation we had in our lives. It carried great weight with me, because he kept at such a distance from all of us. He never offered advice. And I did ring Rob, the Thursday before the Saturday we were to have married. I did say to him that we were only doing this because the worse our rows were, the bigger the gesture of reconciliation had to be. We didn't go to the registry office. We went on our honeymoon anyway. But we never married. Years later a fellow we'd known around that time passed me in a street in London and, recognising me, ran back. "Where were you the day of your wedding?" he called out. "We were all in the Wine Lodge with your presents."

There is another document from the patriarchy I would like to enter here. Someone told my granddad—who was in the Hospice for the Dying—that I had got engaged. As I had; Rob had run out from Doheny & Nesbitt's pub and bought a proper diamond ring. It must also have been mentioned that Rob's grandfather was a "Sir"; he had been knighted for his war work. My grandfather sent me the following letter:

Dear Nuala,

I have just heard of your intended marriage, and deplore same. Do you realise what you are doing—you are marrying out of your own circle, a chap who has no religion, and in a registry office. Apparently you have nothing in common. By your foolish action you are letting down all who are dear to you. What will your friends say in marrying in a registry office a pagan who I predict will show his true colours after a short time together. He will probably have you keeping him. There are I am sure plenty of his likes in London. I would strongly advise you to see your confessor or clergyman whom you must know and lay all before him. It would only be half hour to you now, but later a pain that may be yours during life, if you go on with this and bring shame to your father who is so good to you. Please send this to your titled gentleman postponing your mad adventure and as every cloud has a silver lining this might not be an exception. Now, don't come near me again until you have put your house in order.

Your sad Grandad.

10

I used to walk along the winter streets from Merrion Square, and leave my washing in the launderette, and go up and talk about the novel to a class of night students at the People's College in Ballsbridge. There was a hunger then, as it came up to the 1970s, for self-development. A desire for a second chance at education was part of the massive social change that was taking place.

In Britain, when Harold Wilson was asked what was the most important achievement of his Labour administration of the 1960s, he said, "The Open University," and although it was irredeemably unglamorous, providing "distance learning" opportunities for the masses was a right response to the spirit of that time. And Wilson planned the Open University with generosity. A lot of Labour politicians were personally familiar with the old adult education scene: cold halls, study notes mimeographed onto cheap paper, men and women trying to improve themselves in run-down libraries. The Open University was going to have glossy colour printing, comfortable summer schools on the best campuses, and, above all, it was going to have television and radio programmes made by the BBC to the highest standards of the BBC.

I was so used to England that I didn't think of it as a significant move when I applied for a job at the BBC making Open University programmes. I believed in the OU's mission: I saw it as an extension of what I had been doing at night in the lecture theatre in Earlsfort Terrace and up at the People's College. When I got the BBC job in 1970, I went to live in London. Rob had a little house in Clapham. We still might get married; I wore my engagement ring. There was a cat called Furriskey. I thought we would be very happy.

The BBC trained us in a labyrinthine building across from Broadcasting House, which had once been a hotel, and its winding corridors, its offices that still recalled bedrooms, its false walls and unexpected cupboards and bathrooms with baths and back staircases made it more like a surreal playground than a place of work. It is a hotel again now. I went and stood in its glittering foyer recently, in affectionate memory. We were trained exactly as if we were going into a mainstream department of the BBC. But we were to be teachers as well as broadcasters. I would be one of a team working out the components of a course on, say, the Renaissance or, say, the nineteenth-century novel or, say, the religions of the world. Around me there would be academic experts on literature, music, political history—all the disciplines that crossed in the subject. My task was to isolate the idea or theme or place or person within the subject matter that would best suit being treated on television or radio and best serve the student by being broadcast rather than written or said. Academics are inclined to believe that a lecture—with subject matter such as would impress their peers—delivered straight to camera by their good selves is a well-nigh ideal use of broadcasting. The BBC member of the team, however, had to try to win support for a programme idea which would be, certainly, academically worthwhile but which could also engage an audience used to sophisticated television.

I liked the experience of being trained. I had never been before—and I never was again—part of a group being led to a goal through exercises and competitions and various strategies of induction. I liked belonging. And then, the BBC was a glamorous organisation to me, redolent of Elizabeth Bowen's wartime novels of Portland Place and Regent's Park, and of black-and-white films about heroically restrained men and women with Vaseline tears in their eyes. In the pubs around Fitzroy Square, damaged geniuses back from the war had written radio scripts on the back of pieces of paper. The BBC struck me as being more like Oxford as I had imagined it would be than Oxford itself had been. It was stately and hierarchical and proudly separatist. On one level our training was about manners—about becoming a BBC person. Old Corporation gurus came in to talk to us about ethos. The protocols surrounding bounced cheques were explained at length. I began to sense the extent and wealth of the ancient BBC civilisation, to which the coming of television had merely added provinces—to see how the BBC was a parallel world, with its own buildings all over London and Britain, its own libraries, insurers, doctors, travel agents, lawyers, chefs, grandees. We ourselves, sitting in our training room in 1970, were almost a parody of a new era. My friend Tony was the son of a Ghanaian fire-eater, and he was himself a marine biologist who already had a gland in a certain sea snail named after him; being a scientist was almost as new in the arts-dominated producers' culture we were entering as being black. Some of the other trainees were social scientists, mathematicians, chemists. There was one Scot and one Welshman. I was Irish and a woman. It was confidently assumed that we would become assimilated to BBC ways, not that we and what we represented would in any way change the BBC.

For my first exercise on the course I did a dramatised account, full of thundering Widor organ music and slow dissolves of the Richmond portrait of Cardinal Newman, of the moment when he knew he would have to go over to Rome. Then I did an exercise about Elvis Presley. (I faded to black and played a recording of a foetal heartbeat, running it into the first few chords of "Heartbreak Hotel"; I was awarded zero marks as a result, because if a BBC screen ever goes to black for long it will trigger the deployment of the national emergency services.) I had knowledge and imagination. But I didn't even listen when we were being taught the technical side of television studio and film production. If I heard words like "focal depth" or "interneg stage" I stopped trying to understand. This turning away from even the possibility of acquiring technical understanding and technical skills did me—and a lot of other women, I imagine—great harm. It was cultural. Men were assumed to be capable of learning about cameras and lighting plans and transmission frequencies, and so on. But it wasn't purely to do with gender. You see a shying away from technology, too, in men with poor or bookish backgrounds. My problem wasn't quite one of self-confidence. I limited my own intelligence by refusing to take pleasure in abstract problems or in information that had no human content. The BBC is, or was, so structured that the producer sits at the apex of a pyramid of technical people, each trained to do his or her job as well as possible, for the sake of the job. A producer can be carried, most of the time, by this structure. I was. But technical insecurity is a constant strain, and in the end it limits your thinking. I was stacking up trouble for the future.

I did love the training course. But what mattered most to me was my life with Rob. And it was going hopelessly wrong. For a while we would be happy. He worked at home—he was writing two books, one on Keats, one on the Pre-Raphaelites—and in the evening he'd go up to the tube station and wait for me, and we'd saunter down our street, looking over the fences at all the little gardens, before putting a packet of Wall's First Choice sausages on low in the frying pan and nipping out to the pub next door for a few drinks and a game of bar billiards. We had friends and a set of matching knives, and I was doing the occasional book review for the London *Times*, and he would show me how to do the second draft better than the first. But neither of us knew then how to live with another person. For a while I went in to the training course with a black eye. Sometimes—in bewilderment, and because we drank—we'd attack each other physically. We would say horrible things to each other. I was frantic because he liked another woman very much. She was a beauty, and quite grand. I got prescriptions for the sleeping tablets my mother used, not realising that Mandrax were barbiturates and I was addicted to them.

No one ran the unhappy house. The cat ran away. I came home once from a trip and there was a little piece of desiccated orange peel on the papers on the table and there was dust in the arc of the piece of peel. Where had he been for the last few days? I became expert on cigarette butts, on the charred shapes of things that had been burnt in the stove, on letters that he took straight to his desk. One winter night I went to a country town to see the other woman. I sat across a pub table from her, as my taxi back to the station waited outside. She was a very nice woman. What was she supposed to do? she said helplessly. She was certainly going to go on being his friend. What did I expect?

Anyone who has known jealousy will know how all-enveloping it is. I lived in a bubble of it. I could get out of the bubble to work, but then I was trapped again. For a while I didn't even see the world. I didn't notice the curtain going up on Northern Ireland or anything else. I was very thin and shaky. And heartsore. We must both have been heartsore. In the end, I left.

For the next few years I worked for the BBC in an Edwardian people's palace—Alexandra Palace—on top of a hill in a park. On All-Ireland football final day, Irishmen went up there and put their transistor radios up into the trees and strained to hear the commentary from Croke Park. The Open University section of the BBC moved like a pygmy tribe in the vast dim spaces of the palace. There was a whole crumbling plush-and-gold theatre behind a door. There were high, echoing halls full of forgotten scenery. There was a grey pond, with battered rowboats you could rent by the hour, and the vestiges of a racecourse. It was a dramatic place to work, and the work we were doing was as fascinating as a drama to us. We producers working in the arts faculty of the OU were pioneers, and we talked all the time about the programmes we were making or wanted to make or had been prevented from making. We watched each other's rough cuts and made suggestions and wrote bits of script for each other. My colleagues were very talented. I wasn't in the same league. I said that to one of them, not long ago, when I bumped into him at a conference. "I wasn't very good," I said humbly. "No," he said, "you weren't. But you were a facilitator. You made other people good."

There was a feel of the eighteenth century to the terraced houses and wide pavements and little railed-off greens around the Angel, where I lived. The bus to work rose and fell and rose after it passed the Arsenal football ground, following the contours of the north London hills underneath the crust of the city. The bus the other way descended to a plain. It was easy to imagine the streets as lanes, full of carts going down in the West End. I passed the graveyard where Shelley made love to Mary Godwin on the grave of Mary Wollstonecraft, halfway down the hill to Euston. I'd be hurrying across the square of grass there, on my way to the Open University at Milton Keynes, when I'd hear my own accent. My countrymen, my countrywomen, reeling and nodding, their faces swollen purple with alcohol and rough living. When I saw Brian Friel's play *Dancing at Lughnasa*, that's where I saw the two aunts who went wandering in England in my mind's eye: in the dreary park outside Euston. But I hardly ever thought about Ireland.

I travelled, by myself. I went to Prague, for instance, when not many people did. I got a bus to Lidice. I knew its name; it had been a village razed by the Nazis in retaliation for an assassination. It was autumn when I went there. There were no other visitors, at all. But the man running the place made me sit in the cinema and watch, alone, the film the Nazi camera crew shot themselves, as a warning to others, showing the village being tumbled, the men dragged away to death, the women and children herded out separately, dogs being kicked, and hands with guns jumping into frame to shoot dogs in the head. All in rushing, half-lit black-and-white. Silent. Then I went to the museum. There was a wall of letters—kept, efficiently, by the German postal services, because they had never been delivered. They were from the children to the mothers. The mothers had soon died or been put to death in the camps. But the children didn't know that. *My dearest mama, if you could send me some bread. . . .* I remember that I sat afterwards to recover on the concrete rim of a dry flowerbed, where a few roses had shrivelled in the autumn frost.

I travelled for work. It was a modern thing to have to learn to do, and for a long time I was bad at it. Losing boarding cards. Taking subways in the wrong direction. Not understanding how to use the phones. I was always nervous. I got used to the sensation of being held back in hotel bedrooms by fear of the difficulty of going out. Of picking up the phone and then running out of confidence. But I had to conquer these incapacities, and, gradually, I did. I conquered the gypsies around the station in Florence in winter, and the shared taxis that won't stop to let you out in Teheran, and the men who followed me to my bedroom because I'd been talking to them in the bar of a hotel in New York, and the dust and the heat of a village in Israel where no one would speak, and the time my front tooth fell out when I had to record an interview in the morning; had I not been reading *Jane Eyre*, and had Jane not been so brave, I would have succumbed to panic. I see women with briefcases in airports now, and it is as if they are a different breed.

Sometimes, I banged the door of the flat behind me and set off for the airport. To go to Florence to collect the material to re-create a Renaissance wedding festival; or to the USA, to record radio talks on Mazzini or Courbet or the role of concrete in modern architecture; or to Israel, to film the Passover among Yemeni Jews; or to Scotland, to show how its physical fabric reflects the social history of Gatehouse-of-Fleet. In Cornwall, I recorded the English poet Donald Davie, standing in Hardy's places, giving an eloquent Englishman's reading of Hardy's poems. On the parapet of Thoor Ballylee, Professor Denis Donoghue of New York and Dublin talked about Yeats. I went to Stanford for Rodin and Paris for Tolstoy and Lyons for the revolution of 1848 and Jerusalem for the Greek Orthodox Easter liturgy and Edinburgh for the man who had known the poet John Cornford before he went to the Spanish Civil War. I met scholars and visited libraries and slide collections and galleries. But there were also the hard, slow, frightening bits. I had to haggle with officials; to cope with difficult camera crews, and strikes, and transport that didn't arrive, and demands for cash on the nail, and lonely hotel rooms and boring meetings and airport terminals late at night with the last plane gone. And bad ideas that turned, humiliatingly, into bad programmes. You paid with every bit of yourself for the job, but it was full of revelations.

One moment stands out from those years. It was a remark about music—or, rather, it was prompted by music—and it was said quite casually, one night at the opera in Covent Garden. It is important that it was made by Arnold Kettle, who happened to be the Professor of English at the OU but who more relevantly was a central figure in the Communist Party of Great Britain, and a colleague of the big international Communist leaders and of James Klugman, who had brought Guy Burgess and the other Cambridge "traitors" into the party. Arnold had given everything a serious man could give to bringing about revolutionary socialism. He and his wife were also passionate opera lovers. And I had been listening to opera myself, ever since I found a box of records of Maria Callas in *I Puritani* in a carved wooden chest, like treasure, in a little medieval house I lived in in Oxford.

This was my first time to see *Fidelio*. Arnold and Margot had seen it in Lisbon, the very night the Salazar dictatorship ended; the soldiers in the plot of the opera, when they had come onto the stage that night, had had red carnations in the barrels of their guns, like the real soldiers of the "bloodless revolution" out on the streets. In the first act there is a quartet, "*Mir ist so wunderbar.*" The four protagonists come down to the footlights, and they do that thing that happens in opera—seemingly unaware of each other, they each sing their line of music out straight to the audience, as if it is not of their doing that the lines intermingle in a complex and perfect harmony it takes the four of them to make, but is a separate thing from each of them. I was transfixed, as I always am by ensemble singing. When the curtain came down on the act, I wiped the tears from my eyes and I said to Arnold, "Why is ensemble singing so beautiful? What makes it move us so much?" And he said, "People would be like that all the time, if they could."

This remark was full of meaning for me. It was about his communism, I thought. He must have had in his mind a vision of people perfected—society perfected, free of deformations and oppressions. People so freed would communicate perfectly, as they do when they sing together in opera. Music prefigures whatever there can be of human and social perfection. There is an ideal perfect shape behind the appearance of things. There is the possibility of perfect communication, and to try to establish social justice is a way of moving towards it.

In my real daily life, however, idealism was something quite destructive. It manifested itself as a nostalgia for, or a hankering after, something better and other—something more overwhelming—than even the best things that actually happened. I used to get formlessly depressed. I felt I was not in life, I was looking at it. I'd come back to the flat after being away somewhere. I'd push in the door against a drift of junk mail, and the place would be emptier than empty. The air would be thick. I'd push up the window, and dead brown leaves would rustle down from the lemon-geranium plant. I didn't like thinking about the past, and I had no enthusiasm for the future.

11

It takes a novel to describe the subterranean shifts in the relationship between two people. My friend Tony from the training course and I must have seemed well suited from the day we met at the BBC. We used to tell each other our troubles, lightly enough. He cared about his family. He was the eldest son, and he felt responsible for the others—including his parents—because though they were gifted and beautiful, they lived on a sad housing-estate, and things didn't go easily for them. He would talk about them and about his girlfriends. I'd talk about Rob. But there was a little event that changed us to being real friends, not long after we met, and it was as unpredictable as an invention in a novel. We went skiing, on a Ski-Train to Austria, and I ruined my part in the holiday by getting horribly drunk on the way and then injuring my leg the very first day. Tony was an athlete. He could ski at once, and he looked wonderful, blue-black against the glittering snow. I just hung around, limping.

Then, one night in the hotel, we started taking about poetry. Tony is a scientist. No one had ever taken a poem and analyzed it with him. He wanted to know how that is done. So I jotted down Wordsworth's "A Slumber Did My Spirit Seal" and started to show him how I saw it saying what it says. I remember the warm room: the rough golden wood of the low ceiling and the check curtains drawn against the snow. He sat across on his bed and I sat on mine and I did the one thing I could do— I gave him a vivacious tutorial on lyric poetry, Romanticism, Wordsworth's "Lucy" poems in general and this little poem in particular. That he immediately and totally understood made this a shining episode to me. I valued myself; the self-disgust I felt at the drinking and the clumsiness was alleviated. And I valued him enormously, the seeking intelligence inside him whose prompts he always followed. I trusted him after that, even though what had happened wasn't about trust.

I followed him to a new part of the BBC, which had decided to set up its first ever "access" television unit. The idea was to have an ordinary terrace house instead of an office and to staff it with a handful of non-intimidating people, who would help individuals or organisations who felt overlooked or slighted by the BBC to make their own programmes. These would then be broadcast in a slot called *Open Door*. We applied to work on *Open Door*, and of course we got the jobs. The middle-class, middle-aged white men who ran the BBC not only could not communicate with members of the public, they didn't want to communicate with them face-to-face. There was some kind of confused thinking about minorities going on, certainly. There were two bosses and three working producers on that first *Open Door*. Both the bosses were white men, but the producers were me, Irish and a woman; another woman; and Tony, who is black.

The access idea as it was then was largely a piece of empty rhetoric. Professional broadcasters can hardly bear to put out material as bad as it almost always is, when it has genuinely been made by amateurs. The unseen hand of professionals was everywhere in *Open Door*, picking which applicants got a chance, manipulating the applicants, balancing one sort of material against another. The whole idea was a typical mid-1970s nod in the direction of democracy by an élite organisation just smart enough to have felt the winds of change. I became very doubtful of the value of what we were doing, as we went along. I thought we left a wake of baffled and aggrieved people behind us. The stress of making a programme caused awful rows in groups: I remember an obscure poetry group in Brighton—the mildest of people—eventually coming to blows. The process of examining themselves so as to plan a programme showed up all the things they had been covering over. Individuals, too, never seemed much happier after they'd said their say than before. They still felt misunderstood.

But the idea behind the whole thing was right. I liked the informal style of it, too. I crossed London in the morning on the rickety old Metropolitan Line and came out into the street market at Goldhawk Road and went round the corner to an ordinary-looking house with a front garden, which was the office. I had splendidly bizarre clients. I made a programme with a rich accountant about overpopulation, he looking steadily into the wrong camera as it went out, live. I made a film protesting against pornography with the Queen's gynecologist and his colleagues in "The Responsible Society." I made a film with a religious sect whose meetings I had to go to in a pungent basement lined with mauve satin, where the adherents prayed into a battery, which their leader then took—in conditions of some luxury—to California, where he went out in a yacht and lowered the battery into the San Andreas Fault, so that the prayer-power would seep into the very fabric of the planet.

I made a film for transsexuals. One of them insisted on showing me her new vagina, in her hot little flat in Roehampton. It was a kind of hollow, lined with the skin from her former penis. She had been a policeman in South Africa. Another of them was a gentle Yorkshire woman who had been sent down the mines, when, as a boy, a breast had started growing on one side of her chest. The mines were to toughen her up, make a man of her. She'd tried. She married, and her wife had children. But lovemaking gave her migraine and vomiting. The wife, very understandably, left, and the children lived with their "Mum," whom they sometimes called "Dad" without noticing. There was also a melancholy electrolysist, and a woman who had become a man—an Italian waiter, to be exact. When I took the men who had become women into the BBC Club in Shepherd's Bush they loved going in the Ladies. But they did things subtly wrong. In front of the mirrors, they'd hoick up their skirts to fix their tights. I'd never seen born women do anything like it.

By far the most important programme I made was in Derry, for the Bogside Community Association—the effective negotiating body for the Bogside at that time—after the British army had moved in to end the "Free Derry" standoff. I knew nothing about Northern Ireland; I had been in Derry once, for one day, when I was twelve. But because I was Irish I got the assignment—just as Tony would have got Turks or Somalians because of the colour of his skin, though he was born in west London.

When I went to Derry I saw for the first time a town in the process of being ravaged, and I met for the first time people completely alienated from the state that was supposed to claim their allegiance. It is a measure of the English establishment's ignorance in 1973 that an account of the grave political and social revolution in Northern Ireland, and its life-and-death war, was being handled by a nobody from the tiny "access" unit. But it was an extraordinary experience for me. I was like most foreign reporters; I was thrilled, not horrified, by the place. The bullet-marked high flats, the patches of waste ground swept by fleeing boys after impromptu riots, the terraces of tiny houses in places like the Brandywell where mutual defence had only welded the people more completely together, the slow river, the armoured cars and helicopters and soldiers running backwards into laneways behind burnt-out buildings, the people living on their nerves—I had never been anywhere so exotic.

And so impressive. The Bogside Community Association had men in it—women were not at all noticeable in those early days—who had evolved under pressure into activists of a kind I had never imagined could exist. Paddy Doherty was the most visible individual in the organisation at the time, but there was almost an over-supply of men of intelligence and passion. The BCA had a Portakabin which was on one level an incubator for ideas about the organisation of society. On another level, an old lady might come in looking for a community activist to put in a lightbulb for her. Children came to call their fathers home to their tea.

I had no right to be there—an uninformed person, sent by an uncomprehending institution. I had power over the representation of these people. But they weren't yet known, much less respected. Only through *Open Door* could they even get their voice heard. I did make a film for them—working out of BBC Belfast—that caught something of the intensities of the place. Gunfire broke out across us when we were filming one day. This was commonplace. Yet BBC Belfast was an outpost to the BBC that had been mouldering away for decades. Some of the people there had been beneficiaries of the lifeless status quo in the province. They were quite unable to rise, intellectually or even physically, to the demands of the new situation. They hated everything that had happened since 1969 anyway, and they either couldn't or, in protest, wouldn't raise their levels of competence.

I noted these things, yet when I went back to England I didn't go on thinking or learning about what I had seen. It was just another exotic war, like Vietnam or Algeria. When I went back to Northern Ireland two or three years later, I was still as ignorant as most English media people. I had moved on from the *Open Door* programme and was now working in a general educational part of the BBC. I was given the chance of making two Irish film "portraits." One was to be of Crossmaglen, and one of the Shankill Road. This was for a series that was to be about ordinary life in places that, seen from London, were on the fringe—Scotland, Wales, Northern Ireland—though words like "fringe" were tactfully avoided. These were the last programmes I made for the BBC. Again, I unpacked my bag—in the Rio Guesthouse, Crossmaglen; in the Windsor bed-and-breakfast, Belfast—and walked out to start making decisions with nothing but the names of a few people I might talk to and the eyes in my head. And of course this wasn't enough. There was no ordinary life in these places. But you couldn't explain why there wasn't without going into politics, which it was my explicit brief not to do. I had no option but to make the most noncommittal of films. They looked terrific. Tanks reared through the heat-distorted air behind burning gorse. Silver motes of dust danced in the air where the sun came in around the shutters of a Shankill drinking club. But since they hardly touched on politics, they were like those old cinema travelogues on Bournemouth, gone mad. Not that I fully realized that, then.

When I came back to Ireland towards the end of the 1970s and got a job in RTÉ, I innocently showed my Crossmaglen programme to Nicky Coffey, an old television hand himself and from Dundalk, just down the—highly dangerous—road. I slipped the video into the machine in a corner of the office and went off to my desk behind a partition. I heard him begin to laugh. He was laughing uproariously by the end. He stood up, when the end credits began to roll, and walked off, never saying one word to me. That laughter was the beginning of real watchfulness in me. I paid attention, about the North, after that.

12

Rob and I came back together, in a way, in the tenth year of knowing each other, the same year I worked in access television. All unexpectedly, it was a year of great happiness. I liked working on *Open Door*. I loved time off from work. And the reason for that was a place called Wrabness.

Wrabness sounds Scandinavian. I suppose that Vikings did sail past where Harwich is now and press on up the wide and beautiful estuary which divides Suffolk from Essex. Wrabness was a hamlet on the south bank of the estuary—nothing more than a railway halt and a pub and a few houses, and then a sweep of woods and fields going down to the wide water's edge—a lush and secret countryside, a corner of the most hidden England. Rob had been writing a book on Picasso but he had fallen behind, because he spent so much time wandering London, dropping in a book review here, collecting the fee for a lecture there. So one day his publisher, who was also a friend, told him he'd borrowed a country cottage for him. He put Rob and his cooking gear and his books into a van, and drove to Wrabness, and left him there. He was to stay until he had finished the book.

On many of the Fridays of that year I hurried from work to squeeze myself into a packed tube train to go to Liverpool Street, where I ran through the great echoing station, weighed down by my bag full of treats, and jumped into an express train that went north to Ipswich or Norwich. In an hour or so it came to a junction and I got out, and so did a few commuters, and they'd go down into the station carpark and I'd hear their cars drive away, and I'd be left on the platform in the quiet summer evening or, in winter, in wind or rain. And then the little train would come in that tut-tutted down the branch line to Harwich, stopping every few minutes. It stopped at Wrabness and I'd see, as I waited to open the door, that Rob was waiting in the station yard, beside the hedge sprawling with dog roses or, if it was cold, that he was passing under the pool of light of the streetlamp, hurrying down from the pub at the sound of the train. There was hardly ever anyone else. When the train went off there was only evening birdsong or the noise of a winter night. We'd run up to the pub, and the quiet drinkers in there would look up and say "Allo, Nooly." The nest Rob had left would be there in the corner: his half-drunk pint of beer, his papers and books, the bit of shopping he'd done in the village shop. We'd have a chat with everybody—how the runner beans were doing, whether there was a fête in the next village on Sunday, the pros and cons of getting an electric heater for the bar. It was easeful talk, such as had gone on in that little bar for decades. Lots of the people in Wrabness, even in the 1970s, had never been to London.

Then we'd buy our take-away bottles and head off. We went home by a pathway along the edge of the fields, then by the side of a thick beech wood, and then we ducked into the wood and went across the soft forest floor, parting the boughs until we came out in a clearing in the middle of the wood, and there, in a patch of grass, like a thing of magic, stood the cottage.

Every season was beautiful. In spring there was a sea of bluebells under the sharp sweet green of the new beech leaves. In summer, the golden cubes of straw glowed in the stubble fields and the woods were blackish-green. In autumn, the searchlights of ferris-wheel harvesters played and replayed on the blank wall of the trees as they whirled and thumped up and down the big fields, chewing up whole pea plants and spitting the mulch out behind. Winter was most wonderful of all. First there was a season when the leaves fell so thickly in the wood that there was silence. The mist rolled up from the estuary and the bare twigs of the trees were covered in a cold sweat. Then it would freeze, and when we came out of the pub and started along the path to home we'd be breaking the skin of ice that had begun to form on the puddles when it got dark. We'd turn into the skeletal woods. And there, in its little clearing crisp with frost, would be our cottage, the light glowing from the warm kitchen, the dinner ready in the stove. We had no bathroom, no television, no telephone. We had everything.

Most of the time, nobody came to the woods. There was a deserted stone farm, covered in ivies and brambles, down in a meadow that led to the shore where brown water whispered. Across the wide river, a greensward swept up to the handsome portico of some big house. Those were the only signs of humankind. We were alone with the birds and the flowers and the changing trees. At night, I'd run out into the clearing to pee. If it was winter, my warm feet would melt feet shapes in the powder of frost. I'd run back and snuggle down, quick, quick, behind Rob's back, in the welcoming channel in the centre of the old bed.

We never exchanged a disagreeable word, Rob and I, the year he had this place—even when, one weekend, I came down and found that the clothes and other things I kept at the cottage had all been hidden away. He had had someone else there and not wanted her to know about me. Any woman, I thought bitterly, would have put the things back exactly as they had been. He forgot. I went into the scullery and stood at the stone sink, and for the first time in my life I controlled my response to pain. The place was actually teaching me proportion.

In the end, the owner took the cottage back. Rob had also lost his London house, while he'd been away. We tried to live together in my dark basement flat. It was hopeless. That was when he left a note one day saying *Back Tuesday* and disappeared, and though I saw him again for a while, he never really came back. But what happened afterwards hardly matters. That year of *Open Door* and Wrabness was a culmination. All kinds of accidents had had to happen for it to happen. It wasn't like real life. It couldn't have gone on. But it was wonderful to have it, and especially to have known, while I had it, that it was out of this world.

13

On the first of the huge 1970s marches for women's liberation, young men jeered at us as we shuffled along Oxford Street chanting our slogans. That was how things were, then. Nothing on earth would have stopped me going on that march. But though I knew I needed to be there, I didn't know why. Blatant injustice to women was everywhere, especially in employment, but I had a great job. If someone had come up to me where I stood, in my floor-length hippie coat, and asked me why I was there, I'd have said I was there for other women. It never occurred to me that I needed to interrogate myself. That I'd spent my whole adult life on the errand that smoothed the way to being a woman in the home—a search for a man, for love, for the one man to love and be loved by and have babies with—without *wanting* to be a woman in the home. I could see sexism in operation everywhere in society; once your consciousness goes *ping* you can never again stop seeing that. But I was quite unaware of how consistently I put the responsibility for my personal happiness off onto men. If I'd been asked why I was often unhappy I'd have said, "Oh, I'm having a bad time with X," and mentioned some man's name.

Relationships were the hardest things to think and feel anew. I never joined a women's group, so I never picked up other women's insights.

One remark, made by a sister of mine who was a serious feminist, did give me a flash of self-knowledge. It was a sneer at a—relationship is too strong a word—a one-sided crush I was having at the time. I fondly called this womaniser a "poor man." My sister said, "Poor man, indeed." That was all—but it moved me on.

He was one of two men I had sporadic relationships with during the 1970s that are worth mentioning because they are almost case studies in the limitations of my supposedly raised and feminised consciousness— and in the limitations of any change in man/woman relationships, at least among people who were not young. The first man was not honest or faithful, but he was exceptionally sweet and gentle, and for the very reason that he was so sweet, women—myself included—allowed him to behave in ways that hurt them. The second man was as intelligent and subtle as a person can well be—except in his dealings with women, myself included.

I had met, through an Englishman I knew, a tragic American middle-aged beauty called Peggy Craig, who lived in a big flat in Rome, moving around its rooms in a dressing gown, reading art history and brooding about where her husband, a Hollywood scriptwriter, might be. The husband was an Irishman called Harry Craig, who since he had come up from his father's quiet parsonage in County Limerick to go to Trinity— and probably before that—had been a dedicated, heartfelt womaniser. He was charming, by all accounts, and an idealist—a trade union organiser—and a lover of poetry. He turns up in Maurice Harmon's *Sean O'Faolain: A Life*, helping on *The Bell* magazine: "the assistant editor, Harry L. Craig, a student at Trinity College, who was well known for the lack of order in his life and his sexual pursuits. . . . Craig attributed his success with women to having a double duct in his penis." He moved on to London to cut a swathe through the postwar BBC; he was said to write the Royal Christmas message. David Thomson's widow—Harry had known the "Phoebe" of Thomson's memoir *Woodbrook*—told me recently that the bed in Harry's flat in Hampstead was said to have black satin sheets, which in austere 1950s London was near legendary.

The Englishman and Peggy were close. He and she came up from Rome to Paris once, to the suite reserved for Harry's party at the Ritz, for the gala premiere of *Waterloo*, a film—Rod Steiger was Napoleon—which Harry wrote. Peggy hadn't seen Harry for weeks. But Harry didn't turn up.

I met Peggy in Paris that time. I waited with her in a bar while the Englishman got the car from a distant garage to begin the drive back to Rome. She was a woman of powerful charm when she was well, and she was, that day, and her golden beauty came back for a few hours as she sat in her black velvet coat in the tacky plastic bar. By the time we set out to drive south—I was going part of the way with them—I worshipped her. We stopped that night in Vezelay. It was winter. Burgundy was black as the sea as we drove across it. There was a cold fog in the lanes that led up to the great grey abbey. The village was deserted. I remember that the hotel was in an ancient building, and that we drank a lot of wine beside the fire, and that there was a wide staircase of polished black wood, and at the landing it divided, with narrower flights going to right, where my room was, and to the left. I didn't know which way the Englishman would go, when the three of us went up together on the way to bed. I didn't know what the understanding was between himself and Peggy.

I would have been content to be her friend. I would have been more honoured by her than by Harry's interest. But she was only interested in him. He, as soon as I met him, enrolled me—it was a reflex action—among his lesser women. Then we had to behave like lovers, when we would have been perfectly content to have long lunches. I was less interesting to him than any man because I was a woman, and he knew with weary exactness how to make the low-voiced phone calls, to have the car sent around, to order the Chablis chilled and sent up to the room. Peggy and Harry were unable to climb out of the deep grooves of conventional behaviour, and so was I, even though the women's movement had genuinely begun to change the world.

Harry had such a splendid physical presence, and was at the same time so silly, that he wasn't easily judged. He used to assure us little coven of expatriates who were his guests in Roman restaurants that he was going to do something about Northern Ireland. "I'm going to go to the border! I'm going to stand there and throw my arms wide and say to them, 'Listen!' And then I will read Yeats to them." Then he'd read us the bits of Yeats he was going to read to them, if he ever had time to go to Ireland, with tears of emotion in his eyes. Sometimes it was North African politics he was excited about. He was somehow acceptable to the Muslim film industry, though he drank with gusto. We were enrolled as admirers of Muhammad, of course, and, in modern times, "the lion of the desert"—the Libyan hero of the war of independence against Italy, as depicted by Harry's friend Anthony Quinn. Empathy was his great gift. But it also meant he was a complete moral empiricist. No one could rely on him. His *maîtresse en titre* was an American journalist, and in her autobiography she talks about Harry, and the terrible shock of hearing he was dead, and ringing Marlon Brando to tell him, and how she couldn't stop talking to her mother, obsessively, about her grief for him. The account ends with her mother's judgement on Harry: "I've been trying hard to sum him up, in a single sentence, and I think I've found it. . . .

"He never quite made it."

Harry, in fact, was too personally successful. He implicitly offered the gift of his charm in exchange for being allowed to do what he liked. I accepted this deal. When I was chattering to my sister about how the poor man had to juggle his passports to escape his women and she said "Poor man, indeed," I did see what I was doing. But I didn't want to respond to the feminist call to self-respect. I wanted to know Harry, and the conditions of knowing him were not negotiable.

During those same years I knew another man, a renowned American art critic called Clement Greenberg, who made an absolutely exceptional effort to be honest, but he was no better than Harry at breaking through to some kind of new communicativeness. And I was no more authentic with him than I was with Harry. If intelligence could do it, Clem and I would have had a truthful, intimate relationship. But intelligence seems to have had little influence on premodern habits of self-abasement, furtiveness, falseness.

Clem was old when I met him. He looked very Jewish and very much a New Yorker: He moved his heavy-lidded eyes and his bald head slowly, like a tortoise, and dressed like a bookish Bronx boy's idea of an English gentleman. And he was formidable. In his circles, he was considered a very great cultural historian—this century's Matthew Arnold, even, a lineage he saluted in the title of his collection of essays, *Art and Culture*. He had championed Matisse before anyone else, and changed perceptions of modern painting, and named and promoted the abstract expressionism of his friend Jackson Pollock. He was Rothko's friend and executor, among others. By the time I knew him he was paid to walk around galleries and lend his prestige to the art just by looking at it. He was an immensely serious and original thinker, and in the circumstances of mid-century USA, and the role of art within it, this had made him rich and famous. The nexus of art, art criticism, and wealth to which he was central was later savaged by Tom Wolfe in the essay "The Painted Word." Not that savagery bothered Clem; he was pretty combative himself.

However, when I met him, when he came to the first big exhibition of contemporary art ever to be held in Dublin, in 1972, I knew nothing about this. I just recognised one of those dominant, difficult personalities whose attention it is gratifying to attract. We went off to the west in a chauffeur-driven car with John Elderfield, a young art historian. At Lord Mountbatten's castle at Mullaghmore, Clem bribed a caretaker to let us in, because he had a simple, fervent crush on Princess Margaret, and he wanted to ogle the photos of her among all the photos propped on pianos and mantelpieces. In Galway there was a little show of amateur oil paintings in Salthill, and we went to that. "You'll see," Clem growled to John as we went in, "there'll be more people here with a really painterly feel for oils than in the whole of the States." We went to Cork. "Have you got something kinda acid?" he asked the wine waiter, seriously. "Something that would cut the phlegm?"

I knew him for five or six years and visited him in America and saw him when he was in London. We wrote. He expressed himself with crudeness, but I knew that he was trying to do what he had done in his intellectual life: He was trying "to cut the crap." He continually tried to know himself and to be honest in relationships with women:

How to live? Find out how to let yr. intuitions come through, and how to tell them from the whisperings of the Devil. Some kind of desperation came over me about women. Now I'm in training.

Or again:

Only one out of seven or eight people in the Western world is kosher (which I say flatly on the basis of sixty-eight years of living). But as Kant says you can only find what you look for; something turns over inside you, after a long while, and then somehow you eliminate the un-kosher ones, as many as they are, and more of the kosher ones come into your ken.

He encouraged me:

You'll come into your own. Maybe the longer you delay, the more indolent you are, the better whatever it is you have in yourself to write will come out. The only thing I have over you, I think, is that I've implicit faith in my outcome. But that's only the advantage of a male—certainly in my case, without balls I'd be a cripple.

"All females in the British Isles seem brought up to be petitioners," he wrote. And "in hopes of another orgasm," he candidly signed himself, once.

But I knew, though I couldn't articulate it to myself, that he did not, as a matter of fact, like me. We did not really mean anything to each other. I didn't appreciate him. So why, one winter, did I fly from New York to his house up country, on a snow- and ice-bound lake, where there was no food, and he sniffed cocaine and jitterbugged frantically to the swing music of his youth when it came on the radio, and I was miserable? I went to Edinburgh with him once, and we walked around the National Gallery of Scotland. Hundreds of people would have given anything for the privilege. But I didn't know enough about the history of painting, or have a good enough eye for the paintings before me, to be thrilled by his commentary. And he—for all his "eye"—did he see the living me at all? Did he think I found him physically attractive? Why did he treat me as if I had as much money as he did? He told me to fly from New York to his house upstate; why didn't I say "I can't afford this"? He might have thought I was begging. He mightn't have wanted me at all, if I was troublesome. Above all, how much of an acquaintanceship would there have been if I hadn't slept with him?

The gap between us once visibly gaped. I annoyed him, and he attacked me. "You're a loser," he rasped at me, with pure contempt in his voice. "All you Irish are losers." And he went into a rant full of physical distaste for me and people like me—people (as I understood it) who had no edge, who weren't in the game, who were unimportant, who were soft and melancholy and depressed instead of out there in the bright hard world, fighting towards success. (This is a reaction to the Irish I came across again in other successful Americans. Mary McCarthy told me once that she feared the sogginess of the Irish so much that even when the plane stopped over in Shannon she wouldn't get out, in case she was sucked into the bog. The night Dukakis lost the presidential election to George Bush I watched the results in Boston, sitting beside Murray Kempton, a much admired American columnist and author. "I've never wanted to go to your country," he said to me. "The very thought of it gives me fatigue.") Clem was marking a difference that does exist, I think, between New York Jews and Irish Catholics. But he was marking it with such vigour because he was angry with me. He was enmeshed in dishonesty with me, but he couldn't quite identify it. I know. I knew it then.

Maybe he, like me, knew on some level that we were lessened by each encounter. But it seemed like such a good idea that we should know each other. Maybe he, like me, was pressing on out of a mixture of insecurity and vanity, and out of the desire not to give up—to keep trying things— to go on living and learning. Again, as with Harry, the relationship was too embedded in an old culture to be invigorated by women's-movement thinking. That old culture had come crashing down, but we were wandering among its ruins, picking through its fragments.

14

During those years in London I never forgot the family—the household in Clontarf—for long. I never stood back and estimated them. I called myself in letters "your London branch." I don't remember being surprised, even, when my parents sent my youngest brother to me, for me to get him through his difficult adolescence. He was in trouble with the law in Dublin. My brother wrote to me much later about that time:

> My father suggested to the justice that if only I could be given the chance of vacating the area there'd be no more trouble (for him!). The problem would literally go away. I got to Lime Street Station in Liverpool at 2 a.m. No idea where I was, how to use the phone, what platform, etc. I just panicked, started crying. A policeman took me to the station, cup of tea, calm down, etc.

This brother used to be taken along by my father

> when I was nine or ten to visit Auntie Carmel, who was always "sick in bed." He'd leave me with a young boy in the living-room to play with his train set. It seems vaguely strange to me that (a) I never saw Auntie Carmel and (b) I never sussed the connection

between the young boy and the rest of my family. "Here you are, son—half a crown. Don't tell your mother about Auntie Carmel. She'd only be upset."

This brother hadn't much of a childhood:

> My father was never there. My mother usually drunk. The old man would occasionally come back from some far-flung location and hearing of some indiscretion beat the shit out of me (his army belt, a bamboo cane, his walking stick). Once, after one of these incidents, I stayed out for three days in a cardboard "hut" in a dump at the back of the Clontarf Road. The Ma found me on the fourth morning. "Come home, son," she said, wearily. "Just come home. He's gone."

This brother was an exceptionally gentle and a very intelligent boy— I remember him reading Thomas Hardy, and saying, "He's a miserable git, but I can relate to him"—but he had the marks of neglect on him. I remember the look on a friend's face, when my brother, who was newly arrived in London, stubbed out his cigarette on a plate which still had the runny yellow of an egg on it.

I wish I could have that time back. If it were now, I would push and pull my brother with all my energy towards some kind of goal. But as it was, I was absorbed in myself, and I paid him only intermittent attention. The next few years are punctuated by interviews with bad schools and busts at rock concerts and probation officers and looking for my brother in squats. He was the only important responsibility I ever had. There must be huge amounts of a particular hopeless pain in the world, that no one seems to mention—the pain of someone who didn't do their best for a young person and can never make it up.

Sometime, during those years, I accepted that Rob was gone. I saw him for what was to be the last time for decades at a dinner at St. Antony's in Oxford—it turned out he'd gone back to Oxford—given in honour of

Conor Cruise O'Brien. Dinner was dominated by Lord Goodman, who only stopped telling self-congratulatory anecdotes when Conor forced in an anecdote about himself. Rob and I slept uncomfortably that night in the single bed in his little room. In the morning he walked me to Oxford station. Same place: ten years later. That was the real end of that. But on the level of the incorrigible imagination, I hardly moved on.

I have a notebook that I sometimes wrote to myself in, when I was sitting at night in my flat in Islington, listening to the Third Programme and drinking wine. "If you came the shorter way, across the wheat-field ploughed entirely in October, you walked for maybe three minutes beside the thin hedge of the Old Rectory." I was writing about lost Wrabness. There is the beginning of a short story: a man and his half-drunk wife are hurrying across a field, with their children, to the Christmas party in the landlady's big house. The wife is trying to find out where he has been all day. . . . Childhood was still haunting me.

In real life, I was at a loss. Love seemed to have failed. I went on a binge with another Irishwoman journalist whom I met at a lunch party. We went on drinking, during the afternoon. We found ourselves in a very Cockney, very criminal pub in Kentish Town. There was a house nearby we went back to with men from the pub. I went home the next day, sick, and sick with myself. That was one of the episodes that made me, in the end, hardly go out. Not many people came in.

An Irish writer I knew came to see me one hot summer night and stayed for a few days, lying on the floor of the bedroom, watching Wimbledon. The difference between coming home from work, down the hot street, to him, and coming home to my usual no one! I wrote to that man in the notebook, too: outpourings, full of longing. And full of lies I was telling even myself. I assured him I wasn't needy or lonely. I took a wise person's tone. Even though, the previous Sunday, I'd gone to Mass in Westminster Cathedral in the mad hope of seeing him from the bus, because he lived in that area. Even though I'd have done anything—short of tell him any of this—to have him back.

But I also had friends and suitors. I had two sisters living near me, and I had my brother. I travelled. It was so easy to get cheap tickets out of London that I could go to Rome for the weekend. I worked in Teheran for a few months. And there was the growing light shed by the women's movement.

Ireland and England were in a different relation, in the mid-1970s, than they'd been in even a few years earlier, when I could say intimate things to Rob, or talk to my colleagues at work, without knowing that they heard the accent before the words. Not long before Rob left, the IRA murdered twenty-one people, and injured more than a hundred, in the Birmingham bombing. It was bad enough that, at work, the cleaning ladies backed me up against the wall, in the toilet, and heaped angry questions on me. But Rob turned to me in my own kitchen. "Your friends are murdering my friends," he spat at me. Even though he knew me. He knew I couldn't possibly have known anyone in the IRA. I'd been away from Ireland for seven of the preceding ten years. I knew hardly anyone there, except my family and Sean Mac Réamoinn. I was so uninterested in Ireland—or in public life in England—that I hadn't even taken in things like Bloody Sunday in Derry. I didn't feel Irish in anything, except that I still often went to Sunday Mass. I liked nineteenth-century England: provincial, working-class, football-club England. I knew a lot about England—I knew the literature, for instance, all the way back to Anglo-Saxon. But I knew almost nothing about Ireland.

My old friend Sean Mac Réamoinn came to see me when he was in London. We whipped up his favourite supper of the time: spaghetti carbonara, accompanied by large amounts of sparkling Veuve du Vernay. Sean told me that I must come to the Merriman Summer School on my holidays. He'd helped to found the school. I'd "done" the opening lines of Merriman's *Cúirt an Mheán Oíche*, where he throws off an accomplished description of his native landscape in East Clare, in Irish class at school. "*Ba gnáth mé ag siúl le ciumhais na habhann*," we had chanted. In the effort of transferring this passage to my memory without knowing what half the words meant, I picked up nothing about it. I didn't know it was the opening of a long satirical poem about the lustiness of human beings and their rejection of the Catholic clerics who tried to control them. I didn't know it was by a real person, a hedge schoolmaster called Merriman. Sean had been one of a group of people who wanted to rescue the Irish language from being a grim thing taught in schools and to reaffirm it in every area of life—in comedy, sex, cursing, drinking, everything. These men started the Brian Merriman School so that, for one week a year, anyone who wanted to could go to Clare to learn and talk and listen and sing and dance, in Irish or English, but anyway in the old Gaelic spirit.

It was a turning-point in my life, when I went to my first Merriman. It was 1973. I flew to Shannon one August day and got myself across the county to the grey stone market village of Scarriff, in a mild turquoise landscape of wooded hills and water meadows and lakes and broad reaches of the Shannon River. I had never been in rural Clare before. I could number on my fingers the days I'd spent anywhere in rural Ireland. It was so beautiful, after the grey streets and the dirty tube stations I walked through in London every day. The voices of the people were so expressive. At that school, I fell completely in love with an Ireland which turned out not to exist. Yet this visionary Ireland gave me the impetus to break my links with England. And it pointed me in the direction of the real Ireland I am getting to know now. If I hadn't encountered modern Ireland late in life, and if I hadn't—because of my ignorance and because of being away—thought it was magically interesting, I wouldn't have been so eager to learn about it. And learning about it has meant more and more to me with every passing year. A new concept of "home" came into my life when I realised that Ireland, in all its aspects, present and past, was mine. That I belong to Ireland, just because I am Irish.

The people, mostly from Dublin, who were in Scarriff for the school—academics and artists and journalists and diplomats—were just what I needed. I needed the format of lectures and seminars. It wouldn't have been enough just to have found some lovely little corner of Ireland to go to on my holidays. I needed a crash course in roots. That first time, after so long away, I was shocked and delighted by the lavish amount of personality around. The great bearded figure of the scholar and teacher David Greene is an example of a person who by any standard was remarkable. Soon after I got to Scarriff I was walking along in the company of him and his wife, the sculptor Hilary Heron. She murmured, "Montbretia," as we passed clumps of the slender flame-coloured wildflower twined in a grassy bank. I had first seen that flower when I was eleven years old, when I was sent to a Gaeltacht to try to learn some Irish from Irish speakers. Now, at last, I knew what it was called. That something I had never known the name of was named for me, that first day, is symbolic to me of all that happened because I went to the Merriman in Clare.

The people who were figures at the school seemed larger than life to me. And every event seemed freighted with significance. Liam de Paor was in Scarriff because he was actually living there, excavating a medieval site of pilgrimage on Inis Cealtra in Lough Derg. I went to the site on a wonderful mild and blowy day when Liam had brought a granddaughter of De Valera's, another archaeologist, out to the island, to talk to the students about some of the skeletons they'd found. We went out to the island in a boat and stood in a little bower of green, with the wind stroking the grass, and looked down at the skeletons laid out on the ground. They were very small. One was a skeleton of a woman with the skeleton of a baby still jammed in her pelvis. The De Valera granddaughter bent down to show us our ancestors' teeth worn down to the gum. "It was the chewing on hard grains," she said. "And the honey." That brought them close. I was so moved at being in the sequence: ordinary people who had died in the Middle Ages; de Valera's flesh and blood; and me, allowed to stand there and be part of it.

I didn't see the Merriman people as themselves. I saw them as walking treasures. I was stagestruck. I cried my eyes out at almost everything. I heard for the first time accounts of some of the big Irish songs. I heard Diarmuid Breathnach singing "*Na Connerys*" and a Clare schoolteacher sing *"Sliabh na mBan"* and someone sing *"Príosún Chluain Meala."* There was a late-night club in the hotel ballroom, but it was for dancing. The singing would just burst, you could never tell when, from an individual with a drink in the hand. These things were new to me. I'd only ever come in contact with the traditional Irish arts, and great performers of them, at a couple of Fleadhanna I'd gone to in country towns, more than a decade before. When I was young I'd gone to the pictures on a few afternoons with a lonely Connemara man I met in O'Donoghue's. That was Joe Heaney, the great *Sean-nós* singer. But he never mentioned singing.

I heard people chat away in Irish. Or—better—not even noticing whether they were chatting in English or Irish! These people were like a new species, compared to the Londoners I was used to. They were each so distinct. There was so little grey. I moved in a daze of happiness around the small spaces of the town of Scarriff. I might go to a lecture down in the Tech, or across the street in the little cinema. I might go to one of a number of pubs, for example, Johnny Maloney's pub, where Johnny sat cross-legged at his tailoring in the window, while he conducted a commentary on the affairs of the pub and the nation. I might go a few doors down to Maire Melody's, where I'd be taken into the kitchen for sandwiches of thick slices of ham between chunks of fresh-baked bread. We might even, in the evening, play a game of cards. By the time I stumbled home to my bed-and-breakfast—it was a bungalow so new that they were still digging around it, and every night I fell into a trench—I was a walking swamp of emotion.

I did it all wrong, I realise now. I was much too soppy and gushing for the ironic people concerned. Also, I wore cheesecloth smocks at the time and long Indian skirts and didn't wear a bra. But the innocence of my enthusiasm must have saved me. I thought all the people I met, every single one of them, visitors and locals, were wonderful. I thought everything about Clare was wonderful. We went on a bus trip to Doolin and sat in the sunshine outside Gussy O'Connor's pub, and a girl who'd just won the flute competition at Fleadh Cheoil na hÉireann played. After a week of ecstatic feelings and drink I was poured into a taxi to Shannon, and I wept all the way back to my dreary London flat and for days afterwards; and during the year I had to wait till I could go back again, I often dreamed of the golden men and women who went to the school, and of the lovely contours of Clare.

When the venue of the school changed to Ennis, and then to West Clare, I fell even more thoroughly for the county. I began to rent a house south of Lahinch, on the Miltown Malbay road. Some of my sisters and their children started to go there, too. These were our first-ever family holidays. We were there when I heard a thump in the night from my little sister's room—she'd just heard on her tranny that Elvis was dead. (She wrote to her pal first thing in the morning; R.I.P. was inscribed all over the envelope.) We were there when Mountbatten was murdered. We were there when the Anglo-Irish agreement was signed. We go there now. Some of my sisters—I can hardly believe it—are set dancers in London and Dublin. That came from Merriman: I literally never heard of set dancing till I was in my thirties. That particular corner of Clare— the stone and grass, the cattle coming to the whitewashed milking parlour out on the bright windy road past the caravan site, the little beach, divided by the stream that comes down through the boulders—has been the ground on which we now stand, constructing a relationship with Ireland that is more than simply accidental.

I decided to come home, of course, now that I saw Ireland as home. I had bought a small house in a slum in Dublin for £4,000 a few years before. Squatters had been living in it, but they left. I came back to Dublin, after seven years away, with nothing but a suitcase full of letters I had somehow hung on to during this part of my life (and which I've used, writing this book).

I started off my life in Ireland again on the first of January, 1977. I got a temporary job as a producer with Radio Telifís Éireann, the Irish national broadcasting station. In the job, I went around Ireland all the time with presenters who knew all the ins-and-outs of the country. I remember my first time in West Cork, with Doireann Ní Bhriain. I remember, with her in Donegal, going out on a half-decker from Magheraroarty pier to the scoured stones of the houses on Inishbofin, silent and barricaded against the cruel winter. I remember the lordly rocks in Glenbarrow in the Slieve Bloom mountains—the very core of this place lately called Ireland. I remember going down through Kilkenny to Enniscorthy with Paddy Gallagher, stopping at pub after pub, on the trail of the designer Eileen Grey, for *Folio*. Inis Meáin, the first time I was ever on Aran, in spring, had wild flowers in profusion in the cracks of the stone and hens scratching on the grassy street. RTÉ crews stayed in every second-class hotel in every town in Ireland. Bailieborough. Youghal. Birr. Dungarvan. Loughrea. Listowel. Cavan. Each of these names—every name in the country—evokes a whole complex of memories and impressions, has a distinct taste, calls up an atmosphere as definite as a colour.

I was extremely naïve about Irish social groups. The shock of finding that out was, in the long term, a blessing: I'm interested in looking behind surfaces, now. I realised as time went on that the Merriman School, for instance, like most Irish events, had a core of insiders and people perceived to be "important" and a periphery of people perceived to be less important, and that this pecking order was a matter of difficulty and, often, hurt. I saw that the school, as one of the very few venues where adult men and women were together outside their ordinary Irish lives, could reflect the awkwardness and shyness and sudden cruelties that continue to deform social intercourse between the sexes here. I think, over time, that the school changed and that now it is more accessible than it was. And it is less forgiving of "characters." I went into a packed and happy pub, with Nell McCafferty, who is from Derry and a republican, the first night of one Merriman, and a Merriman "character"—a history professor from Cork called John A. Murphy—sent over a note saying *No Provo-lovers wanted here*. I don't forgive him for that. I don't forgive myself for fawning on the same man later in the evening to get him to sing. I don't blame the Merriman School, of course. It is valuable exactly

147

because it is one of the few events in the year where opposites—Northern and Southern, nationalist and unionist, being one—do meet in a social setting. But it is not an easy event, on many levels. Nothing that attracts so many egos could be.

RTÉ wasn't easy, either. Going around the country was one thing, but working back in headquarters in Montrose was another. The same larger-than-life personality I admired in Irish people compared to English people was a burden if you had to negotiate with it day after day in colleagues. Yet it was an immense exhilaration to come back from England and be free of its rigid class structure. It was wonderful to be with people who were what they were, not cowed and classified from birth. At the BBC in the early 1970s, when I was working on location, the technical staff ate at a different table from the producer and presenter. The electrician might be called "Sparks" instead of by his proper name. It was an enormous relief to be away from that. But an agreed social hierarchy, such as there is in England, helps organisations to work smoothly. Some of the people in RTÉ, compared to the BBC, seemed to want to be charmed or amused or pushed by superior force of will into doing their job. They were brilliantly good at it, often. But doing it well for its own sake didn't satisfy them. If they were bored, they'd obstruct everyone else, and if they were in a good mood they'd help with unsettling lavishness. And there was the usual problem of men who disliked working with women. This was expressed in a particular Irish way. Women were put down by endless recall of the golden era of RTÉ television production where "great nights"—usually drinking escapades—had been had by this or that group of men. It was being made clear that the present situation was a comedown.

Women were also excluded by the rough, macho management style often in play just underneath the good manners of formal management. The place was run by men—not all of them nominally bosses—who had "strength." The "strength" would be personal or political, hardly ever professional. Some producers and managers didn't really know what they were doing, technically speaking. But they didn't care. Real passions were ideological or political, though these are words too grand for the very limited aim of the dominant ideology, which was to keep anyone with any sympathy for Northern nationalism as far as possible from any influence.

I've heard it said that RTÉ television hasn't come into its own, so to speak, because its development has been checked by the Troubles. But other organisations in the media—*The Irish Times*, for example—developed perfectly well, while covering Northern Ireland in a competent and honourable way. In RTÉ, two things connected with Northern Ireland seemed to me to be happening. Direct public, personal abuse of anyone deemed to be either nationalist or insufficiently antinationalist was allowable. Meetings about Section 31 of the Broadcasting Act, which censored nationalists, were particularly vile. Perhaps it was because RTÉ television is such a young organisation, but there seemed to be no governing standard of professional or personal conduct. The second effect of the energy poured into antinationalism was that no programmes mattered except political and current affairs programmes. In the BBC, people of energy and talent worked in arts and features. In RTÉ, those areas were often moribund.

I myself benefitted enormously from a different aspect of those times—the new interest in women. In the 1980s, I worked a lot on women's programmes. I did a series, inspired by the way the audience participated in the *Late, Late* and other chat shows, called *Women Talking*. Doireann Ní Bhriain and I went around the country and sat down with almost random collections of local women and recorded the ebb and flow of the talk as they discussed subjects that interested them. Then I worked on *The Women's Programme*, where Clare Duignan and Marian Finucane and Doireann and I did pioneering pieces on incest, prostitution, abortion, women's pay and employment, contemplative nuns, health issues, Unionist women and their views on Southern women, the fall-out within their families of the activities of "supergrasses" both loyalist and republican (protest from an antinationalist to management about that—we shouldn't have included the republicans), world issues for women, the Hormone Replacement Therapy debate, how to run a 10K race, where in Ireland there are the most unmarried men (Ballaghaderreen, County Roscommon, at the time), and so on. It was serious, and it was fun.

Nell McCafferty used to do a marvellous script about women in the week's newspapers. She would take something—for example, an ad for thermal underwear, based on testimony from a priest about how comfortable he was saying Mass in this thermal underwear on various mountain peaks—and she'd weave an extravaganza from it. Between the five of us, we were approaching women's issues from every angle and in every mood. At a European Community weekend conference once, in Brussels, on women and broadcasting in the EC, after Clare's report from Ireland—which included *Women Today*, then running on radio—broadcasters from all over Europe came up and congratulated us. They thought RTÉ must be really progressive. And it was a place where opportunities could suddenly appear. This was the good thing about the lack of hierarchy: A person could take an idea to a manager, and if the idea was good and the manager a powerful enough patron, they could cut through the usual structures and make their programme. That's how I got to make the series on older women called *Plain Tales*.

I started and ended my RTÉ career on "magazine" programmes. These are the ones whose titles no one can ever remember; they go out early in the evening and consist of four or five harmless items described by reasonably good-looking presenters sitting on sofas. These magazines cost a great deal to produce in terms of human effort. The last one I was on had people like Cian Ó hEigeartaigh, who is a true scholar and aesthete, and Richard Crowley, an exceptionally gifted newsman, and David Blake-Knox, a real expert on television comedy, and myself, and perhaps ten other production staff, all churning out six-minute items on things like female bodybuilders. It isn't easy to manage Irish talent. A lot of people who work in RTÉ are almost by definition dissatisfied. I was. It was a stroke of the greatest luck, to get the chance of going to *The Irish Times*.

. . .

By then I was well on my feet. But the first few years back in Ireland from London, the years leading up to 1980, were in most ways my life's lowest ebb. I was back with my family again. I couldn't cope with physical things. My basic lack of skill in directing in the television studio kept me terribly anxious. I was frightened all the time. I couldn't light a gas cooker because of the *plop* of the first flame. I couldn't go to the dentist, I couldn't climb a ladder, for fear of heights. And I was unskilled at everything. I couldn't drive. I couldn't type. I didn't know how anything worked. My house in the slum was beyond me. A big grey rat jumped out of the clothes press. Plaster fell in chunks from the ceiling. I had never run a house, and even hiring workman after workman, things got worse. I didn't understand Ireland. One summer afternoon, when I was in bed, four or five big men shouldered their way in downstairs. They were Special Branch, they said. They wouldn't talk to me as they began going through my bag of coal and taking up the floorboards. Then their leader saw that I had some books in Irish. "Can you read Irish?" he said, obviously impressed. He stopped the search. I didn't know that they couldn't do that—they couldn't just walk in and push a citizen around.

Things happened to me, at that time, instead of my choosing what would happen. The worst was getting pregnant. I was thirty-nine. I was so completely stunned by this turn of events that I was quite unable to think about it. When I miscarried, quite painfully, all one night in a room by myself in Holles Street Hospital, I still didn't know how I felt. I still don't know.

You can never get everything together, if you're drinking too much. You can only do a bare minimum of things. But there are also good sides to drinking. A pub always has a company of regulars. People who drink in the afternoons belong to a company of people who also drink in the afternoons. Pub life is an undemanding, floating way of life, unjudgemental and full of small incident. People who are as shaky as I was then are very kind to each other. I had thin relationships with other people who drank too much. I was never well. It was hard enough coming to terms with RTÉ, but it was a self-imposed handicap, doing that on a diet of hangovers and take-away Chinese. My former friend Michael, with whom I had discovered sexual bliss when I was twenty, took me out a few times. But we had nothing left to say. I was just going through the motions, with the relationships I had.

Yet that seemingly waste time just before I was forty, when I was on the edge of alcoholism, was in some deep way rewarding. An aspect of being vulnerable is that you are very open. I used to lie on the bed and look at the sky as it very, very slowly got dark on summer evenings. There was a kind of perfection of melancholy. On Sunday mornings, or on Bank Holiday weekends, I had absolutely nothing to do but feel the quiet. In a way, I was with my self very fully. Afterwards, I used to miss that feeling of being held within pure, empty space.

I thought nothing was happening, then. But my head was filling with riches. The mosaic of the country was being assembled inside it. The mysterious valleys between Leitrim and the sea with the oily black rivers full of fat trout. The stretch of plain—deepest, silkiest green—out beyond Lissadell, with its abrupt end at the fierce beaches, as indifferently beautiful as when the little curled ships of the Armada foundered on their rocks. The Shannon welling up silently into its round pot and then changing character, discovering youth, prancing out towards Dowra to begin its long slide down the country. Down through the silvery-greys of the water meadows, down past what were stone hotels, corn mills, old canal buildings, past the swans waiting beside half-submerged alder trees. In winter, when you get the train that crosses the Shannon River, it seems to go across the surface of a huge water into low country. In the wintry light, the train goes into the water, and the water is steel and carries the train. But Ireland isn't just landscape, but history and present society. There was famine and brutality and emptiness in the country. And the damaged underclass I was part of in the afternoon pubs was as much part of Ireland as its beauty.

15

Most memoirists in Ireland write about their fathers in a sweetly one-dimensional way, as if there were no unconscious. The older man I knew when I was a young woman—the doctor who helped me get through college—was wary of my relationship with my father. He used to hint to me that my father preferred me semi-derelict—that when I found strength, for example, to take my mother for help without his knowledge, it threatened him. But I wasn't aware of anything except that my feelings about my father were (and still are) contradictory. I feel a pang, for example, every time I remember that the last he knew of me was those drinking years. He'd be so proud of me now. Yet I also believe that it is not a coincidence—though there were other reasons—that I started getting healthy when death took him, and a few years later my mother, away from me.

The others, my sisters and brothers and even my mother, must have been as ambivalent about him as I was. No matter how, on paper, he most certainly let us down, he didn't abandon us. We mattered to him. And none of us could ever be even for a moment genuinely indifferent to him. Just when you thought it was safe to hate him, he'd make some loving and sensitive gesture. He was particularly kind to the daughter who most resembled his own mother: my sister Deirdre, who married young, is a truly religious Catholic, and who with her husband has reared a large family in a modest and happy home. The thought of that household must have often comforted my father (as it has all of us). Daddy visited Deirdre in the hospital when she had her first girl after three boys: A hand came around the door, holding a silver cup, then another hand, holding a bottle of champagne. That was the sort of gesture he'd make for any of us. But he offered Deirdre, in particular, steady important kindness. He was a different father to each of the nine of us. Some of us hardly had parents at all. Some, when my father was getting older and milder, used to have a lavish supper and play cards once a week in the small flat he and my mother and my little sister, the last of all the children, had ended up in. Not that Mammy played cards; she wafted woozily in and out of the bedroom in her nightdress, looking like Miss Havisham.

One of the things that tormented my mother was that my father would tell her nothing. She never knew what exactly the financial position was. A few times the poor woman even went into town and, trembling, braved whoever his paymaster was at the time to ask that his money be given to her directly. Nothing was ever sorted out. His life was ideal for concealment. No one felt any obligation to her.

She did get some leverage when my father sold the only house he had ever had a mortgage on, as opposed to renting. He murmured, "Your mother really cannot be trusted with stairs," a remark calculated to win him sympathy for the step forced on him by her drunkenness. But in fact he was in some kind of worse-than-usual cash crisis. He moved my mother and my little sister, who were the only family members he still took responsibility for, into what turned out to have been the flat of his mistress. She, presumably, had been moved somewhere else. My mother discovered this one quiet night when she was alone, reading in bed, and the mistress burst through the bedroom door and attacked her with the bedside lamp. It would be funny, if both women hadn't been so desperately unhappy.

I gather from Michael O'Toole's reminiscences that my father's mistress was a public fixture. O'Toole refers to my mother in half a sentence as a very intelligent woman who had a problem with drink, but goes on to tell an anecdote about my father's companion of long standing, who was apparently well-enough known around town to have a nickname: "The Lady." I didn't know the mistress was well-known until I read O'Toole's book, and I was shamed for my mother. The anecdote had to do with my father arriving at an antiques fair bleeding from the head where the mistress—apparently unable to hold her drink—had attacked him in the back of the car. The man from the welcoming committee was lost for words at their appearance and asked my father—for something to say—whether he was interested in antiques. My father makes a quip about never travelling without one.

I can't say I find this funny. But I do admire my father's fast thinking on another occasion. Mammy told me, when my little sister was born, that Daddy had visited her in hospital and suggested the baby be called Carmel. "Carmel?" my mother said. "Why?" "I've always had a devotion to Our Lady of Mount Carmel," he told her. I knew, though my mother did not, that the mistress—I presume the same one as in Michael O'Toole's anecdote—was called Carmel.

After the bedside-lamp incident my mother got herself to Clontarf garda station, where she received first aid and prepared to lay charges against the mistress. My father came hotfoot from whatever part of town he was gracing. He begged my mother not to disgrace them all in public. In exchange, he offered her information. She would know how much he earned, how much he owed, and how much he'd got for the house in Clontarf. She settled for that.

He was a very disciplined man, and extremely reserved. The public carry-on with Carmel, if it was Carmel and Carmel did hit him, was a decline in his standards. The years of trusting no one but himself must have told on him. He had no partner, no peers—no friends, when it came to it. The day he could not, finally, go to his work, he made his own arrangements. His driver was waiting outside to take him on the usual social round. He was too weary to knot his tie. "He sat thoughtfully awhile on a stool beside the phone," my sister wrote in a letter, "little finger hooked between his teeth, head tilted sideways as though listening." Then he picked up the phone and cancelled his appointments. He booked himself into hospital that day and packed his own bag and went in there for good.

My sister Deirdre recalls how my mother and he reached for each other, at the moment he knew he was going to die. My father had leukaemia, and on a certain day, after two months of horrible chemotherapy, the consultant was to say whether the treatment had worked. "At 3 o'clock the consultant arrived up at the far end of the floor and proceeded on a leisurely tour through the wards," my sister wrote:

> Isolated inside Dad's room, we chattered desperately in low voices while we waited, petering into silence when we heard his brisk steps approaching. There was a slight pause, then a quickening of his gait, as he hurried past the door, down the corridor, then clattered down the stairs. My father's piercing blue eyes opened wide and caught Mother's brimming eyes in his. He stretched out his hand to her. Neither spoke. Some time later, my dad chuckled wistfully and, turning his face to the wall, embraced the waiting coma.

We "children" were not so important in those last months. But my brothers, in particular, whose young lives he had made desperately hard, threw up everything to be near him in the hospital. I understand their still reaching for him. I don't understand his neglect of them. I see fathers all around me, and they love their sons with a practical passion. But my father dumbly refused the ordinary effort of being a father. My brothers were loving and bright, but there was no tolerance for the difficulties of their growing up. One of them was no trouble, but he was almost punished for that and let sink into unskilled casual jobs, where he wasted years of his life. One of them, after a saga of desperation, had ended up starving in the England to which his father had bought him a one-way ticket. He joined the British army, which hurt my father as deeply as anything could—the man who had changed his name from his parents' anglicized Phelan, to the native O'Faolain! Yet my brother did it in part to impress him, being too young to know that nostalgia for the Irish army was quite a different thing from being pleased that your son is a squaddie. A sister who was only a teenager, working as a bank clerk, tried to promise her wages in advance to raise the money to buy the brother out. My father said he would buy him out, that when a certain insurance policy matured he would pay the sum necessary. But nobody bought the brother out. And then my parents deported the youngest brother to me in London. My mother was drunk when she put him on the boat. My father wasn't even there.

How do you forgive these things?

My father acquired a companion, Frank Finn, late in life, a large, benign, almost completely speechless man who for a couple of years went everywhere with my father. When Frank died, I wrote a letter of condolence to my father. He replied:

I find it impossible to believe in the living and the dead and the resurrection, though I stand up in St. Gabriel's and say all this. Another surrender of reason is due, I suppose. Unreasonable is the thought that there is no point in looking forward to the resurrection and the life unless your friends and neighbours and all you loved on earth are there . . . but that to me conjures up a vision of a non-stop press reception . . . for all eternity . . . and I don't want to interview my grandfather who was an RIC sergeant and who left me his eyebrows, or to be interviewed. . . . We buried uncle Frank dacent. He had no next of kin and he left me all his massive wardrobe. I gave it to the Men's Night Shelter in Tara Street and the Norfolk Home for Unfortunates and some gigantic tramps and drop-outs are now magnificently dressed by O'Callaghans of Dame Street. . . . As you will understand, the loss of Frank Finn hurts much more than that of my brother. One was a lonely man all his life, and I know that towards the end . . . this huge and gentle man depended on me as none of my children did, and I am glad I was with him every night till a few hours before he died with dignity.

My father is telling the truth here. He did love Frank. But the phrase leaps out at me—that Frank needed him "as none of my children did." My brothers needed him. We all needed him.

At the end of his dying of leukaemia, when he had shrivelled and discoloured and was like a terrifying brown boy, hunched in his nappy on the mattress of his bed in the hot room, we still looked up to him. It was terrible to all of us to lose him. My brother whom he had not saved from the British army came home and joined the vigil in the tobacco-smokey room at the end of the hospital corridor—even though this brother had been tormented, in childhood, by the sounds of my father beating my mother. And even though—and he said in a letter afterwards that it hurt him still—"on at least two occasions, when I was a child, my father forgot my name."

There was nothing we wouldn't do. I went to Confession for the first time in twenty years, to prepare for a Mass beside his bed. My brothers and sisters didn't sleep, didn't eat. I could not read, for the only time in my life. I went back over and over to the same poem, the Tenth of the Duino Elegies, where Rilke praises suffering. "We wasters of sorrows!" he says:

How we stare away into sad endurance beyond them,
trying to foresee their end! Whereas they are nothing else
than our winter foliage, our sombre evergreen, one of the seasons of our
interior year,—not only season—they're also place, settlement, camp, soil,
dwelling.

This elegy, and the last part of Mahler's "Lied von der Erde"—I had the Kathleen Ferrier record—forced themselves on me. I'd go back from the hospital to my cold house in the slum, not wanting anything on earth and too tired and sober to dramatise myself. But these two pieces of work did quite straightforwardly console me. They are both full of perceptions—vague but compelling—of ultimate meaning. The promises of Christianity meant nothing to me. This German romanticism was all I had to oppose to the anguish of pity I felt for my father. That God wouldn't let him keep his aloofness to the end, but forced him to beg, "Take me out of here, take me out," his eyes becoming round and filmed exactly like his mother's when she was very old. "Just take me home." On his gravestone we had carved, "*Ar ball, gheoamíd radharc, aghaidh go h-aghaidh.*" In the end, we will see, not as through a glass darkly, but clearly, face-to-face. I don't expect, of course, to understand life and death. But I might understand some day what kind of a father my father thought he was. What kinds of fathers there are.

He was very lonely. And my mother was lonely. But I think they had a middle-of-the-night understanding that only they knew about. She often boasted to me, shyly, of what confident lovers they were. Perhaps she felt she was altogether there, when they made love. Perhaps sex was her best experience of wholeness.

I was at a horrifying Sunday lunch once in a house in Hampstead, with the actor Robert Shaw and his then wife, the actress Mary Ure. He abused her loudly and steadily from the beginning of the meal. If anyone said anything, he, watching her all the time, would say something like, "Do you hear that, you stupid woman? Are you listening to what intelligent conversation is? Or are you too stupid to know what an intelligent conversation is?" After five minutes or so she ran out of the room, choking with sobs. He relaxed immediately and began to tuck into his meal, smiling cheerfully at us shell-shocked fellow guests. "Sorry about that," he said, "but I have to do it. She doesn't know she exists unless I put the work in."

The arrangements between my father and my mother were almost as hard on us, the bystanders. They would be cruel to each other. Then, for no reason we knew, they'd forget that and get on well. For decades, he referred to Mammy's drink problem as if it were a wryly amusing habit of hers. He took her on holidays and faced down the criticism he must have encountered. Silently, he would not allow us to discuss her with him. When she was falling down in the street! Getting sick in public! It was a vast denial. But it kept a kind of dignity possible between them. "Oh, Katherine! I've always loved your smile!" I remember him flattering her with his last strength, in his hospital room, not many weeks before he died, even though to anyone else her smile was a half tranquillised, half terrified rictus.

After he died, she looked around absently for him, the way you might glance around a room if the light in it suddenly changed. Every so often, my sisters would with heroic effort get her into a home to dry out for a while and get some treatment for her malnutrition. Mammy was like a child in there—afraid of the authorities, keeping clear of the other patients, hiding in her room, lonely as ever. She would ask me plaintively, "What's wrong with your sisters? Why is everyone so cross with me?" She didn't even remember the awful episodes my sisters were dealing with all the time. And she'd say, with honest petulance, "*Why* did your father die and leave me here?"

She didn't even totter down to the pub anymore. She stayed in the flat. She kept the amount of time she had to be conscious as short as she could manage. When she got up, sick from gin and sleeping tablets, she would start drinking again. If she got her doses right she could be slack-faced and unreachable by late afternoon.

I drove out to see her every week or so. I would ring beforehand, my stomach cramping. I often put the phone down, halfway through dialling. But then I would work up my courage again, knowing that if I was lucky I'd get her in the interval between her being too sick to talk and too drunk to talk. If she seemed lucid enough on the phone, I would hurry out to the flat. Sometimes she was ready for me, sitting on her chair in her crumpled coat, her handbag clutched to her chest with pallid, shaky fingers. In my relief my heart would open to the pathos of her.

The lipstick swiped on with unforgotten expertise. The blobs of mascara. The dabs of pink powder. When under the makeup her skin was grey, and bristles were breaking through on her upper lip.

If you fed her the cues for one of her little reminiscences going along in the car, and if you linked her up the steps into the library, and the librarian quickly got her four or five books she would like, and if you sat her then at a sunny window in some hotel lounge with a double gin, she would radiate happiness. She would take on the mannerisms of a pampered, pretty woman. She would beam, in a blurred kind of way, at any people around. The flowering might last half an hour. An hour.

One Sunday I phoned before going out to her. She seemed all right. But she didn't pick her way to the door to unlock it when I rang the bell. I stood on the doorstep, afraid she was dead. I went around to the window and peered through the slats of the blind. She was sprawled on the floor. Her legs were wide. She was snoring. She wasn't dead. She was dead drunk. She had her coat on, so she had been ready for me, but she had overdone whatever drink it was she had glugged down or whatever pills she had gobbled from her palm. I stood outside and banged and banged on the window and shouted at her to get up, get up! raging with grief and anger and furious with a lifetime's fury at her doing this to me.

Soon after that, I was driving to the West, and as usual I was writing her a letter in my head. You did this, you did that, you didn't do that. . . . And suddenly I felt a single sharp sensation: the vibration of a single heavy twang. And it was the parting from her. It was completely unexpected. Breaking-point. From that moment on I was at a little distance from her. So when a few years later she intimated to me that she was going to die soon—though there was nothing particularly wrong with her—looking up at me as I stood at the end of her bed and giving me a wonderfully frank smile, when she said, "Nuala, this can't go on," I just said, "That's right." I admired her from the bottom of my heart at that moment, looking down on her poor face, all discoloured by falls. She was at her stoic best. She wasn't looking for sympathy, or even comment. She was merely remarking, in quite good humour, that she was finished.

When they rang me a few weeks later and told me she was dead—that she had died in the bathroom, and they had found her on the floor—I was almost prepared. I had seen her sprawled on a floor. Her dead body was only the same as the body that had shut me out, that day I shouted at her through the window.

I remember her through windows. Standing at her bedroom window when she was young, a sheet wrapped hurriedly under her ivory shoulders, in the bungalow we lived in then. She was shouting at us children to go and play, to stay out, not to come in till we were called. Then she turned back into the bedroom, where my father would have been waiting.

She left her clothes, one ring, and an estate which totalled £1000. She left the biscuit tin, with her scribbled book reviews in it, and the letter from my father, from Donegal. And she left us nine people, her children. None of us had mattered very much to her. Once, when we all happened to be in Dublin, six of us adults got together and took our courage in our hands to go and see her and ask her to allow us to get help for her. She threw us out of the flat with a few venomous words. We were only "the children."

One of my younger sisters lives in a town down the country, and not long ago the women there organised a "Woman's Day" and I went down to report on it. "I'll have to go to a workshop for the morning," I said to my sister when I bumped into her in the crowded hall. And my sister gave me a glimpse of herself—I hardly know her—when she said, "Well, I'm going to one called Adult Children of an Alcoholic." It was extraordinary to sit beside this sister in a circle of women in a small room, with Mammy back from the dead between us, in all her power. At one point, the woman running the workshop asked everyone to draw the floor plan of the house they had grown up in. I drew the flat instead, that our mother died in. Two little boxes of rooms, and the bathroom where liquid gushed into her lungs, and the breath was choked out of her, and weight bore down and down onto her heart until the last beat could not labour on, and life emptied out of the empty thing on the floor.

In the workshop my sister and I said almost nothing. The most terrible stories were being told by some of the others. When we came out after the morning I said to my sister, "She wasn't that bad, was she? Compared to what some of those in there had to put up with, we had it easy. Didn't we?" But my sister just looked at me, and turned away, and left me to hear for myself the eagerness in my voice. And the falseness.

16

There is one broken-down hotel in Mopti, a little Malian river town on the Niger, on the edge of the southern Sahara, thousands of miles into Africa. Nell McCafferty and I had stumbled off the ten-hour bus from the capital, Bamako, when it got into Mopti in the steaming, insect-humming dark. The boy who had carried our rucksacks from the bus didn't want us to go to the hotel. It was *trop cher*. So it was: In the dim foyer with its empty display cases a woman got up from the tangle of staff lolling on mildewed sofas for long enough to give us a key and tell us the unbelievably expensive rates. Fleets of velvety green frogs scuttled before us as we felt our way down a dark path to our room. They hopped against our door. Inside, the erratic air-conditioner dripped water on the floor and stirred the air in the stagnant room. The concrete walls were covered with smears of dead mosquitoes. We had not been able to eat the brown messes the other bus passengers bought at roadside stalls, but the hotel had no food. I had been sick all day from a reaction to anti-malaria tablets. We turned out the light. The heat thickened. Odours of mould rose in the terrible little room. Dogs howled outside. The night was going to be awful.

We lay on our stained beds, sweat trickling down our faces. I heard

Nell light a cigarette. Then she said out of the dark, "Do you know what?"

"What?"

"I don't care what Bishop Casey did. He shouldn't be made to stay in the tropics. They should let him come home."

I did the planning of our holidays. I had great ideas—we were in Mopti, for example, on our way to Timbuktu. I'd heard the phrase "from here to Timbuktu" all through my childhood, and Timbuktu was the most exotic place I could think of. Now, for Nell's fiftieth birthday, I'd surprised her with tickets to go there. But my ideas would often land us in trouble, and I'd fall into despair. Nell kept us going then. She pulled laughter out of the hat. We were in the Peloponnese once, living in a hut on a beach, just north of the Mani. The first day we set off to walk through olive groves to the village, not realising how hot it was. After a while we were panting, purple in the face, hardly able to breathe. I was afraid I'd collapse. And then we saw a water trough, with a pipe trickling into it! We threw ourselves into the cool mud around it and soaked ourselves in the water. When we finally crawled upright, our hair and clothes stuck to our bodies, covered in mud and moss and leaves, Nell said—as one writing a caption to a photo—"Irish models take a break from the catwalk."

She never blamed, no matter what we got into—bamboozling a travel agent in Bologna to sell us train tickets home on an expired Access card; being threatened by Serb men we'd been drinking cherry brandy with in a hotel bar in Belgrade; trying to climb a glacier in Norway with an ice axe, because the man in charge of our walking holiday liked to frighten. There wasn't anything Nell couldn't lighten. Even after Timbuktu, when she was rushed to the fever hospital with life-threatening malaria, she stopped me being tragic. Half delirious, with a temperature of 104 degrees, she managed to whisper, as they were putting her into the ambulance, "For my sixtieth, I'll arrange the surprises myself."

But I don't know whether we'll be in touch on her sixtieth birthday.

We lived together for nearly fifteen years, and it was by far the most life-giving relationship of my life. I had always admired her as a brilliant journalist and a fearless campaigner for civil rights, north and south of the border. I came to love her. But we were made helpless by our angers, in the end. I don't know why. In *Hamlet*, when the ghost of his father comes back to harass him, Hamlet jumps from spot to spot, bending his ear to the ground. "Art thou there?" he calls. "Old Mole!" he calls, trying to pin him down. The old moles of my childhood come, malevolently, to the surface of the ground I try to stand on.

When I was a child, in Athlone, once, there was a festival on. The song of the day was "On Top of Old Smokey," so it was that year. There was to be a parade, with music and fancy dress, and then soft drinks and sandwiches in a hall. The thing is, I was a helper. I was a trusted lieutenant. I wore myself out in an ecstasy of helping—running here, running there, carrying messages, tacking up crepe paper—being responsible, being part of the indescribable glamour of it. I remember running down the rainy street, past the lights of the shop windows to the hall where the lady I helped would be needing me. I've never been absorbed in anything as much again. That is my ideal. That is what I imagine good relationships are like. But I have never wanted to help a partner, since I grew up, with my whole being, the way I wanted to help that lady.

Deeper than heart, primitive feelings would stir, when Nell made any real demand on me. Why can't she look after herself? I don't ask her for anything. And if I'm not asking her for anything, why is she asking me? I mind myself. She can mind herself. I hear that voice, and I think, I've heard that voice before. Is that not the primitive hostility my mother expressed in her drinking?

Our two lives became involved with each other around the time my father died. I was physically and mentally at the end of something. I went into St. Patrick's psychiatric hospital on the morning of Christmas Day, in 1980. We had buried my father a fortnight before. I was in shock. I had hardly slept since his death. I had nowhere to live, either. I'd sold my little slum house sometime that year because I couldn't cope with it.

A friend was putting me up. I wasn't easy to have around. I drank all the time and couldn't get drunk. In the end I asked the friend to get me into hospital, and he did.

It was exciting, that breakdown. I thought I was having huge insights. I kept scribbling writings down that I was sure would be of the utmost importance when I had time to study them. I was swept with tides of emotion. I lay in my bed one night, listening to the rain on the window, thinking of it lashing onto my father's new grave on the hill in Sutton and seeping down on to his lonely corpse, as I wept for myself, in the guise of weeping for him. Then I heard his voice! His voice! Someone on the radio murmuring in the corner had played a tape of an old interview with him, in memory of him. I was a mourner ambushed. Thinking of his voice, silenced, reminded me of all the voices that had been silent all their lives, down the centuries. I wept for the millions and millions of anonymous women who might never have been, for all we know of them. I wrote a kind of paean to them. I still couldn't sleep.

But Nell came back from her family Christmas in Derry and a friend lent us a place in Sandymount, and I began to mend. She was exactly as ready to bustle bossily and warmly and unself-consciously into someone else's life as I was not. She looked after me. Slowly, I began to drink less. I ate a bit. Six months after I met her, I threw away the last of the sleeping tablets. I remember one glorious spring morning coming out of the flat and going down onto the sand and dancing with the purest delight.

I began to be able to stand back and see the world and manage it a little. I tried to buy a solid little house, even though a mortgage was hard to get at the time, because I didn't have a permanent job. I did have a job, though: I was teaching, on a year's break from RTÉ. One day, I had to go to a man in the bureaucracy of the place I taught in, to ask him for a letter saying that though I was not on the staff, a permanent position might ensue. I needed this letter quite desperately; if I had it I could get a mortgage. I believed that if I had a house and my clothes were hung up, I could sort myself out. This man had a big office. He sat at his desk. I sat opposite. He looked at me with open contempt. "What makes you think you'll be kept on here? I have no evidence that you have performed your duties satisfactorily. I'm sorry, my dear, but I am certainly not signing any letter." And so on and so forth. He gloated, because my employment record for the year was so bad. And he knew how to do it—he'd been on top of the heap, because he was a middle-class man, all his life. I crawled to him. I had to, to get the letter. When I got home, I was glad to be living in an all-woman household. (And I often was again.)

I went back to RTÉ, this time to *Féach*. This once-powerful Irish-language programme had a complex history, and its standing in RTÉ was a complex matter. So much I understood; otherwise I was an outsider. I didn't mind. I'd become like most workers; the real focus of my life was my home. I could hardly believe it. We had a house. We went to a sale and bought dishes. I couldn't believe how rewarding order was, and cleanliness, and making a home. Once I came back from a few days working down the country. Nell was all hot and bothered. She had a towel wrapped around her jeans as an apron. She had been making pizza dough and had it in a bowl in front of the fireplace, and it wasn't rising the way it was meant to. I had never known anything like this simple crisis. It gave me the deepest pleasure. I never wanted to go to a pub again. I felt as if I had come in from being on the road almost since I was born. I felt we belonged. We knew a couple who were equal friends of the two of us. When they had a little girl we were the joint godmother. I planted a white lilac in the little square of earth outside the front window of the house. On the first warm Saturday of that summer, our first year, we sat out there, eating our breakfast. An old lady who lived further up the cul-de-sac leaned over our gate and said, "It's lovely to see people enjoying themselves. You're very welcome to the street." The more we made a life that was regular and ordinary, the more I was freed. The public world became my interest and entertainment, because my private world was secure.

Yet Nell and I were not alike. We didn't agree on very much. It was only when we were abroad that we relaxed with each other. On our holidays, the rough edges of our personalities were smoothed. We were never more than tourists, but we were that with the intensity of travellers. We went to the Communist-run European countries, not knowing that the Iron Curtain would one day be raised. Because those countries were cheap, we could leave huge tips. The old women in cloakrooms used to kiss us. We had duck and black cherries and a whole gypsy orchestra in Gundel in Budapest, and a box at the opera, where everyone applauded the arias so heartily that the singers repeated them, even if they had to come back from being shot or stabbed to death to do it. We went east, and the thunder and lightning caught us out walking across the endless Hungarian plain, and the sky turned black and cracked open and we held on to each other crouched into the earth as lightning crackled around us. Outside the austere Calvinist meeting house in Debrecen the first refugees from Romania were gathering; borders were becoming porous. When we came to the wide river that divided us from the Soviet Union, Nell stood on the gravelly bank and sang, to the thick woods on the other side, "Lara's Theme" from the film of *Doctor Zhivago*, to show that we were friendly.

We got to know Iron Curtain food, before the Wall came down. Dry pork. Balls of gristle. In Warsaw the gallant people—the women so dainty in their homemade frocks—got up from the tables and danced to the shabby band, while they ate the bits and pieces of cheap meals. In Prague the people in the packed Christmas streets talked in such low voices that there was a surreal absence of noise. We were the only people having Christmas dinner inside the perfect marquetry box of the panelled dining room of the Europe Hotel. We wore our coats. The kitchen had made a great effort, for those times. There was a little pattern of gherkins around the meat. The waiter was as cold as we were. We propped our books on the ornate table silver and shivered.

Prague was sad, but in Budapest, another Christmas, we heard the people answer back to Moscow, at Mass in the cathedral. There were soloists from the opera and players from the orchestra up in the balcony, and after the service they had bounced the "Hallelujah Chorus" off the great dome of the church. And then, the congregation—the solid men in their belted loden coats, the women in neat astrakhan hats—had launched into a hymn in Magyar, singing it out with such fervour that we knew it was their equivalent of "Faith of Our Fathers." We came out so affected that we had run, half laughing, half still crying, to pull ourselves together in the Ladies of the Hilton.

We heard the first sounds of the end of the Soviet empire. We were in Austria, cycling down a stretch of the Danube. Hungary had begun to allow East Germans to get out across its border, and their road to West Germany ran parallel with the river. At night, when the countryside was very still, we would hear the rattle of the overloaded Trabants as they—the first to be released from the socialist experiment—made their way to new lives.

"This is the life," one of us would say fervently, settling back in the chair in a café in the warm Mediterranean night air. The feeling of lightness: the being freshly showered, lightly dressed, at leisure. Lobster and candlelight on the quay at Fethiye. The lunch we had every day at the two-table café behind a scraggly hedge in Sperlonga with little golden chips and greenish ice-cold wine. We'd be just finishing the wine when the afternoon shower would come, and we'd run across the road and peel off our T-shirts on the rain-pitted sand and *whoosh* down into the foamy sea through the warm rain. We went into a fin-de-siècle tobacconist shop where they sold loose oval cigarettes wrapped in old sheets of Arabic newspapers, in Aswan, and hired a barouche pulled by a malodorous horse, and ate ice-cream in the street, smug at our adventurousness compared to the English belowdecks in the cruise ship, moored on the exquisite Nile. We swam unexpectedly in our bras and pants in the turquoise Atlantic waves that rolled into a rocky cove near Lisbon. We walked through the hot dusk, in a village south of Kalamata, to take our ouzo and saucer of titbits at the outdoors taverna where the men of the village argued and laughed under lights strung from the plane trees, and flocks of noisy birds rose and fell from tree to tree as they tried to settle, and the election vans went up and down playing tinny music. "This is the life," one of us would say.

Fleeing the video bars east of Corfu, we took the boat across the Adriatic to Ancona, to go up through peach orchards to arrive at last in the honey-coloured stone piazza in Urbino and watch stately parents and their tumbling infants, out for the evening stroll. We got drunk on hot sake with the proprietors when we were the only people in the Chinese restaurant, in Ely, on a freezing New Year's Eve, when we were wandering a deserted and beautiful England. The ilex woods above Spoleto, the sushi bar in New York, the rushing green river that went down to the fjord in Norway, dancing *paso dobles* in the seedy ballroom in Barcelona, eating a trout in Salzburg because we knew the name from Schubert, swimming in the hot springs full of classical debris in Pammukale— "This really, *really* is the life." On a slope of scree in the Agrafa mountains in Greece or when I was frozen by vertigo to the edge of a ravine in the Vercors, Nell talked to me and got me through. She showed me how to be courageous. When I got tired she told me the plots of films to keep me going the last few miles: *The Magnificent Seven, Bad Day at Black Rock.* In Rome, she knew the Colosseum already from the movies: "Victor Mature came out of that archway there." In Sicily we could see Don Corleone everywhere, even in the businessmen having lunch beside us in the chic café near the Fountain of Arethusa, where we ate pasta with cream and shrimp in January, fifteen years after we met, the door open to the sunshine and the boisterous sea. I said, "This is the life," tentatively, that day, but we couldn't smile, because we were leaving each other.

We would come home to Ireland, close. Then the messages, the tensions of free-lance journalism, the snapping at each other. . . . Yet I loved the way she always woke up happy, swimming up to the surface, babbling away about her dreams and slurping up, half asleep still, the tea and the bread I'd bring up. I'd hear her singing in the shower every morning. When she was sick, she was so humble. And I'd see her coming towards me in the street, a formidable woman in her jeans and little, worn shoes. Once, she and I went to Belfast for a night and walked through carnival streets down to the docks, where the Tall Ships were visiting, and the whole city had come out to look. We fell in with some

Unionist women who had seen Nell on television—Protestant or not, they knew their *Late, Late Show*. We sauntered along, happy to be together, them interested in Nell, she fascinated by them. They were ahead of me: four or five middle-aged women in pastel cardigans and big beige shoes, their heads turned to Nell, the small delighted one in the middle. Most of us just take what we're given. But look at her, I thought, full of energy and argument, because there are women here to talk to, and politics to talk about. She'd argue with the world. She *has* argued with the world.

In Nell's family house in the Bogside, the visitor would sit on the sofa in the back room, the big telly grimacing in its corner, while her mother wandered in and out from her tasks in the scullery, patting her pinny down, regaling the company with a stream of anecdotes and ideas and tales tragic and humorous and questions about the world and sayings and disquisitions on this and that. I had never met such a charmer. She played on the sofa with her grandchildren and taught them hymns and songs and how to show courtesy to neighbours, especially the elderly, and inducted them into how things are done and were always done. The tea, for example, of "red fish" and great bags of chips, wouldn't be right unless served on the table with sliced white bread and butter, pickled onions, beetroot.

I sometimes came back early to this house, needing a bit of solitude, maybe from a daughter's house to which the whole family—granny, daughters, in-laws, friends, grandchildren—had decamped and were settled talking in front of the television with their drop of tea. I'd fish the key up through the letter flap and walk down the brown tunnel of the hall past the holy water font, into the little ticking room, where the tablecloth was folded on the corner of the table ready for spreading, the mother's apron hung on the back of the door, her slippers lined up under the rocking chair, the cuckoo clock whirring on the wall. I would stand in this rich, eloquent silence, knowing that the family knew where exactly everything was and had always been—this ornament, that bottle of pills, Lily's purse, the Padre Pio prayer card. At first, I sentimentalised it all. Then I felt an outsider to it.

There was one night in particular when the McCafferty family's courtesy mattered to me. There was a debate in the Guildhall around 1994 on the subject of feminism and nationalism, and it came down to a standoff between Bernadette MacAliskey and myself. The hall was packed with a partisan crowd. They were egged on by Bernadette, who prowled up and down on the platform behind me, rolling pieces of paper into balls and flicking them sharply at my back while I spoke. I said feminism was about human development and was therefore incompatible with killing. I said the armed struggle was one of the reasons there was no all-Ireland sisterhood. That Southern women, in my opinion, had little or no sympathy with Northern nationalist women. That the men of Sinn Féin were just another layer of patriarchs among the many in Northern Ireland that oppressed women. That women who lived on tea and biscuits brought steak to their husbands in jail, and the men took it without apology. I bitterly regret making that last insensitive point. But otherwise I bore with being excoriated by Bernadette and by fierily eloquent speakers from the floor. I was spat at on my way out of the Guildhall. It matters a lot to me that when I went back to the little house in the Bogside the McCaffertys were the soul of tact. Because they don't understand why I am what I am, any more than I understand them. We have been formed by completely different historical experiences. Yet they don't retreat into righteousness, and they don't ostracise.

Nell and I disagreed about many things, especially the politics of the island, and after a while we hardly talked about them at all, for fear of fighting. Not many people came to the house. We didn't talk much at home. Gradually, I seemed to myself to lose the ability to talk naturally at all. I didn't notice at first. I liked not talking. But when I got the chance of working on the *Booklines* programme in RTÉ, I discovered that I was so rusty at ordinary communication that I used almost practise how to go into the room where the production team met, and how to talk, because

I had forgotten how to behave in a group. I'd come away sometimes with tears of chagrin in my eyes because I'd got it wrong again—been too loud or too sulky or too flippant. I was ridiculously sensitive to hurts from other people and not sensitive enough to whether I was hurting them. I hardly knew how to sit calmly and let a bit of talk ebb and flow.

Abroad, we chatted about all the little things of each day. We walked from Volterra to Siena one warm rainy May. We stood in under dripping trees while the rain soaked the heads of poppies till they bent, and the bright drops made the banks of violets sparkle. At night, we tried to dry our boots with the hair dryer. One day, deep in a valley of vivid green grasses, we came to a river. "Cross by the stepping stones," the instructions said. The rains had swollen the river far beyond stepping stones. We took off our boots and trousers and put on our runners and waded through, even our panties getting soaked at the deepest bit. And we stayed that way to climb up through the wet undergrowth on the other side, until we came to a village: two half-naked women of a certain age with their legs pink from the cold and plastered with grasses and seed heads and leaves, laughing like lunatics. That night, the two of us squashed into four inches of bath water. We started laughing again, snorting helplessly.

Abroad, it didn't matter that we didn't talk much. We read. We read the same paperbacks at the same time, me speeding along and tearing out the pages as I finished them, for her. I remember in Opatija—which we'd gone to on the coastal ferry from Trieste, because of Nabokov and a story of his I'd once loved—we sat in our hot little room behind the metal *J* of the Hotel Opatija sign and solemnly read a novelette called *The Rich and the Beautiful*, passing each page across. We read all the time, meals included. We read local newspapers and children's schoolbooks and left-behind thrillers in French, if there was nothing else.

In my best memory of the two of us, we are reading: one in a little bed under the slanting wooden roof of an attic, one in a little bed tucked into an alcove opposite. We are in a bed-and-breakfast in Bergen, on our first night in Norway. We have wandered the town, deserted in the soft, implacable rain on this late September night. We were not the rich ones now. We'd stood outside a restaurant, watching through the window as people got a bottle of wine put on their table. "Twenty pounds, minimum," we'd breathed. We'd had a Chinese meal and tea. Now we were propped in our beds, hearing the rain on the roof, seeing the rain sliding down the little dormer windows. Warm and companionable, our Irish troubles forgotten. And surrounded by little lamps. The landlady seemed to have a thing about lamps, and we'd lit them all, and the rain-sounding attic was full of lights and shadows and felt as if it were sailing through the night.

17

And did you get what
you wanted from this life, even so?
I did.
And what did you want?
To call myself beloved, to feel myself
beloved on the earth.

Raymond Carver, "Late Fragment"

I didn't have to give this account of myself at all. I don't know why this story insisted on being told. Partly, I think something was dislodged in me by the evidence given about his childhood at Brendan O'Donnell's trial for the murder of Father Walsh and Imelda Riney and her little boy. His sister told of the brutality Brendan saw: He saw his father smash his mother's false teeth with a blow, and the mother trying to jump from the car, and Brendan screaming at her not to jump. He saw the father's incessant beatings. His mother—who was well until her marriage—broke down. Mother and son huddled together so close that she went to school with him, to stand in the corridor until Brendan could let her go. This evidence wasn't even printed in the *Clare Champion*, the local paper. The waters closed over yet another Irish family. My two brothers in England had their life's chances taken from them in childhood as surely as Brendan O'Donnell had. Maybe that trial brought me into the presence of my own sorrow and anger.

Or maybe that's just fanciful. Maybe what matters is that it was a few days before Christmas when I first thought of writing something about myself. Christmas is a time when powerful feelings are stirring. And this was going to be my first Christmas completely on my own. Ever. There wasn't even a special person whom circumstances had prevented me from sharing the day with. Since Nell and I had parted, there was no such person. I wasn't absolutely alone, of course; I'd be speaking to some of my sisters on the phone, and people would ring me. But I had no person of my own. In my fifties. I kept coming up to this blank fact and looking at it. It wasn't that I was unhappy. But I kept on thinking— sometimes surprised, sometimes just making a note of it, sometimes panic-stricken—"You're on your own. You're on your own."

What happened?

I know this isn't a tragedy. On Christmas morning I was in Clare, driving up the coast to meet a friend who would give me a lift further up, to Ballyvaughan. I was going to spend the day walking back over the Burren to my own car. Suddenly, I heard myself on the radio. I'd recorded a little piece for that morning's *Miscellany* about the wonderful light and colour of Christmas when I was a child, and how that magic had infused the phrase "and may perpetual light shine upon them" for me ever since. And so it has. But my beautiful goddaughter died when she was eight. I imagine her held somewhere in some golden radiance. And the word "perpetual" means that she is gone off into that light forever. For all eternity. Her suffering, her pointless bravery—all for nothing. What she went through, and what was lost when she died—that's what tragedy is. Or my brother, who was sent to me to mind in London so long ago (there's no getting through Christmas Day without going over the family in your mind). He's a grown man now, with a life of his own. But I see a suffering child in him. He ended a letter to me about the pain of his childhood: "I don't blame anyone or hate anybody. Just me."

Just himself. That's tragedy. And he is only one of the Irish who might come stumbling out of England rubbing their eyes if there was a way of taking the past back. And in the world—I'd just a few weeks before Christmas come back from Manila, where I'd been writing about sex tourism and children used for sex. I was still full of all that.

I do know perfectly well that I don't deserve any pity in such a world. And I'd planned the day so as to eliminate creeping self-pity. But why should I devalue what was wrong, either? Millions and millions of people besides me have thought that another person is what you need to complete yourself and to offer completion—that together you can unlock the best of the world and the best of yourself. I was in Holland not long ago, and I went on the train to an open-air museum, with ducks and apple trees and old fishermen's cottages. Suddenly, the most fine rain was borne across the place, on a satiny breeze. I want to be with someone! I cried out inside myself. It is ridiculous to go around open-air museums on your own! I feel chockfull of experience that it is now too late to share. Until I met Nell I had no right companion to marvel at the world with. I heard her footsteps stop, once, behind me on the forestry road above Glendalough. When I went back she was immobile, open-mouthed, looking at a bird smash the snail in its beak off a rock. In Paris, we found the doorstep where the baby Edith Piaf was born. Nell walked away backwards down the street, like a child, unable to pull herself away. I saw things through her absorption in them. I could tell her how I'd seen things when she wasn't there: "The boat to Paros swung in and out of other islands just casually," I might say. "As if it was a milk van dropping a few bottles off."

How brave widows and widowers are! How resourceful people are, and how many secrets they carry around with them! It is not about sex, the desire to share with another person. But it is about creation. Even though what "together" means is a mystery. I stayed in a village in the Pyrenees last autumn. It was small, quiet. In the evenings, in the square outside the church, a few teenage boys and girls played a kind of badminton. They played as the dusk came down, calling out softly, until it was too dark to make out the glimmering white shuttlecock. The event wouldn't have been different if there had been a person with me, glancing out through the windows of the hotel. But it would have been a whole: us, there; it happening. Instead of a fractured thing with me, by myself, knowing that my solitary self was observing this lovely scene.

When I stay with the couple who are my closest friends, I hear them laughing and talking in bed, and sometimes in the middle of the night one of them goes down and makes tea, and when the clock goes off in the morning, they start again, talking to each other.

What happened to me?

My Christmas Day was cleverly arranged. I made luxury sandwiches—avocado and bacon. I packed them and a flask of coffee for myself, and a bottle of water and a carton of gourmet dog food for Molly, my mongrel collie. When my friend dropped us off at the green road that goes around the flank of the hill above Ballyvaughan, the dog leapt and bounded into a landscape crackling with frost, brilliantly bright in the winter sun. It isn't possible not to be thankful with all your heart for such a high blue sky and such a sweep of sparkling valley. How wise I was to be there! But underneath—I didn't believe in my own wisdom. While loving what I was doing, I didn't believe in it. How can I be so sensible? I thought. Will I be able to keep all this positive stuff up? What will happen next year?

What happened, to make contentment so precarious? I've been trying here to understand the way things have worked out in my life. And though what I've written is personal, part of my predicament is general. The challenges of middle age and the challenges of loneliness—which I know exist even within relationships—confront many more people than me, just as the same place I grew up in and the same influences I came under affected more people than me. Teachers used to say, "Miss Noticebox! You're nothing but a noticebox!" But when adults slap children down and tell them not to be drawing attention to themselves, what are the adults doing? Why do they want the child to stay quiet and go away? Single middle-aged women aren't supposed to kick up, either. Who wants to know about them? If no companion depends on them? If they're nobody's mother? Nobody's wife? Nobody's lover? If they're not famous or powerful? My problems are banal only because so many people share them.

The time and the culture I grew up in proposed to me that somewhere in the creation there was another person—my other half—walking towards me. That person would catch sight of me. But a woman past the age where she might be contemplated as a sexual partner is hardly seen. She turns into a silhouette. Nobody scrutinises her in detail. She could become a "character"—in Ireland, anyway. But being avidly watched because you might at any minute make everyone laugh is a parody of being watched because you are desired. I met two old ladies on a train in California, on the first leg of a long journey. They were on a frank, not to say raucous, quest for husbands. In Ireland you're not meant to mention love, after a certain age. Yet life teaches you to value love more and more. Human love, if you can secure it. And if you can't, you must hope that other loves will bring you through to the end—for a house, or a garden, or a country, or a job increasingly well done, or money, or animals. But how can you confer on those the status that loving a person has?

The dog makes me tender. She couldn't believe her luck that Christmas Day. She'd run up the path ahead of me, and then turn and crouch, looking up at my face in her mild and hopeful way, checking that we were still committed to this heavenly activity. We went along behind Newtown Castle, under the flank of the hill, and then we climbed with the little road up to the ridge where there's an old fort, and we sat among stones glittering with ice and had our picnic. That night, I would look around the room of the cottage: Molly deeply asleep on her back, her legs sticking straight up, her pink tummy offered to the air; Hodge, the cat, staring, immobile, at the flame of the Christmas candle. I love these animals much more than I want to say. But they are not children.

Rob has a child. He rang me from time to time over the years, usually when someone we'd both known had died. "I couldn't go to the funeral because I was picking my boy up from school," he might say, or, "I last saw him when I was taking my boy for a spin on the bike." One day last year when I was in London he asked me to lunch. I wanted to see him again while I still had my own teeth. So I went to his house and chatted in the big family kitchen with him while he got things ready, and then some friends came and he opened bottles of wine, and then his wife came home from her office and was warmly welcoming to everyone, and eventually nobody wanted to go back to work. Then he and his wife bowed their heads to each other in a quick murmur about domestic arrangements. Then she disappeared for a while. I saw that Rob was watching the door. Then—it was as if the density of the air in the room had changed. A small fair-haired boy in a scuffed school uniform hung in the doorway. He lifted his face to his father in the hope that he wouldn't have to say hello to all of us. This person, waiting to be released to run up to the television, was of a different order from us adults around the table. His head, his soft hair, the school tie badly knotted around his thin neck: The more you looked at him, the more you saw why his father would want to mention him in every sentence, would want to say "My boy, my boy." He told us—in a whisper, but confident—that Arsenal would win the Cup. Then his father gave him the nod and he slipped away.

I would have been a very bad mother, during most of my life. But I'd be a good mother now. Too late. Sometimes I have to look away from small children: hopping where they stand as their mothers try to put on their little jumpers, or talking to themselves pressed against the window in the seat in front of me in the bus. They are too beautiful to bear. Then again, I see what is done to them. One year, on an elegant beach in the south of France, I saw a father dangle a terrified little boy at the water's edge, ducking him into the waves. Sometimes, after an episode like that, exhausted by my own cowardice as well as by pity and anger, I think, truthfully, I just want to be finished with everything. But mostly, the life-force inside cries out. The world looks at middle-aged women and talks about sexual frustration. But what is it that has been frustrated? Is it that a woman's life is bracketed by two hormonal tides, and one goes out, in middle age, and she runs down the beach after it? Is it that the children she hasn't had are calling out within her? It feels so like the body asking for something to begin. It doesn't feel like a farewell. People say without thinking, "Oh, what she needs is sex." That would be a fine distraction. But the longing is in the head and the heart as well as the body.

The body is where it expresses itself. A while ago I tapped out the opening paragraph of something I called "novel." There were just a few lines:

Sometimes when she wakes up during the night and straightens her limbs her hands slide across her breasts and she is ambushed by a sensation of their softness before she can guard herself against it. Then she sees herself as if from above. A middle-aged woman under a duvet on a bed in her space on the surface of the spinning planet, pressing a face twisted with the anguish of a lonely body down into her own shoulder. She clenches her eyes in shame, as if there were someone to hear her groan. Sometimes she smoothes her sides and her belly and rubs her thighs with her useless hands. She has a roll of fat around her hips. But she is flexible, still. "I'm still a woman!" she says. "Use me! Find someone to use me. Or let me get old—quick, quick!"

She is pleading, I think, not just for physical excitement but not to become invisible, at least to God.

The remembered fluency with another person, the remembered ease with the self, the complexities of the imagination at last in perfect balance—that's what there is to regret. I went through a time, three or four years ago, when I saw love everywhere. I saw two handsome, middle-aged tourists—Italians, perhaps—in white macs, start to run, laughing, with their arms around each other, when a shower of rain blew down Nassau Street. I saw a middle-aged man I work with drop a kiss on the top of the head of his middle-aged wife as they waited to cross Eden Quay. I wanted someone who had known me when I was young to trace the lines that had come on my face with tender familiarity. And, as well, I wanted to be mad about someone. I wanted more time! And I wanted time to be wiped out, the way it used to be!

Time. I note every day the physical detail of middle age. The transparent polyps that have formed on the skin of my neck. The first white hair in my eyebrows. Pigment spots on my midriff, which will never tan again. I see people my age cherishing their parents. No service they can offer is too much. If my mother had got old and I had been able to love her, would I be able to love my own ageing body now? If I had had children? How do people arrange to love their ageing selves?

How can you persuade yourself to accept your fortune? I was as fortunate as anyone in the country on Christmas Day, and I knew it. We came down from the ridge, the dog and I, slipping and sliding on the icy track, and we crossed the rushing river at the bottom of the valley and then we set off up the other side through crisp, squeaky snow that had caught behind the ruined walls and stands of trees, there, where there was shelter. In that perfect air, we hummed with energy. We were halfway home. As I am. *"Nel mezzo del camin."* And back in the cottage, as darkness fell, I piled turf in the range. I tickled the little circular cushion of velvet that is Hodge and woke him up. I opened the wine. My neighbours saw my light go on and at the signal sent a daughter up with a Christmas dinner to me, on a plate, wrapped in tea towels. I had saved up a Henry James story I'd never read before to have with the meal. There wasn't anyone on earth, as a matter of fact, that I would have preferred to be talking to, rather than reading "Madame de Mauves." I was warm. If I cried at the Christmas music on the radio—well, that's almost what it's for. And I was sleepy; that's why I'd walked so far. I had everything. All I needed was to be able to convince myself that I wasn't pitiable because I was alone. And that there was nothing wrong with having so much.

"I don't want to live like this!" I shouted at Nell once, during a row. "I want to live like Colette!" Even in the crisis, we both started to laugh. I'm no Colette. But I long to pick up some small bit of her gift for living, now, when I need it so badly. Colette was in her seventies when she wrote:

Love, one of the great commonplaces of existence, is slowly leaving mine. The maternal instinct is another great commonplace. Once we've left these behind, we find that all the rest is gay and varied. But one doesn't leave all that behind as and when one pleases.

I can't agree with her (not yet, not yet) that life without love is "gay and varied." The new genre of middle-aged women's writing insists on the delights of the postmenopausal condition. We are to become benign witches. But this is meaningless to me. I went to a talk Germaine Greer gave in Dublin a few years ago, hoping to be inspired by her vision of new access to vitality around the age of fifty. The lecture theatre was packed with women, just as eager as I was, I presume, to listen to someone who spoke to our biological and cultural condition. It was worth going, if only to look at her, because she is so handsome and assured. But she chose, as prima donnas do, to confound expectation. She gave a rather dull academic talk. I want a more plausible prophet. I want to believe that old age is not to be dreaded.

Luckily, in real life, little things make people very content. I see it in the languor with which they answer the door, because they've been curled up in front of the television, or the eagerness with which they reach up to the shelf in a newsagent for the latest *Gardening Weekly* or *The Gramophone*, opening it even as they queue to pay. People do not live in single states of mind. I'm as often happy as not. And whatever it is I am lonely for, it is not for company. I have Yeats's "company of friends" in my head. I have imaginary companions as real as the girls at the Dunnes Stores checkouts or the man next door, coming out onto his step for a smoke. "Bookworm," they used to say at school. That's right. I've wormed my way into what I've read and no one can ever shake me out.

Music is, however, a more dangerous element. It can surprise me, getting at me before I can stop it. Especially the human voice, and especially voices intertwining in sestets, quartets, duets. Voices imploring each other, resting on each other, playing with each other. Even in pop music it is the unison of voices—Dolly Parton and Kenny Rogers, Sarah Brightman and José Carreras—that starts a response. I listen in what Martin Amis would call "a miasma of spinst" to pearlfishers, Madame Butterflies, Rusalkas imploring the moon, countesses grieving for past love. This romantic commentary comes out of the culture around me, reaching for me, trying to ruin me. The trio at the end of *Der Rosenkavalier*, where the older woman gives up on love and sings her line of acceptance and renunciation in intricate relationship with the ecstatic lines sung by Octavian and his new young love, strikes me down with sorrow, every time. Except once, when a small strange cat put its head around the door when it was playing. The cat did nothing but peer in, alertly. Yet it was so other to the music, so here and now—it brought so different a world into the same place as the world of human emotion and human art and human performance—that it distanced the power of the music.

That Christmas Day I had all my resources marshalled. Health. Landscapes. Friends. Food and drink. A book, and music. And my cat and my dog. Those little beings are saving me much more directly than by their company or by being graceful and amusing. They have given me the measure by which I find my parents wanting. I don't like my mother and father, when I think about them and these animals. Hodge sits folded into himself and perfectly still, gazing with narrow golden eyes into the mid-distance—a tiny, plushy sphinx. He has a ball of a head, a body like a plump velvet teardrop, wide and innocent paws, a fat tail, "*Mrkgnao!*" he cries, like the cat in Molly Bloom's basement, when he's hungry. He flops into sleep. "*Eck?*" he says softly, if he half wakes, "*eck?*" "Get that cat out of here," is all my mother or father would have said.

I took it for granted that they had little tenderness for us. They made me accept that, for myself and my brothers and sisters. But I can stop being passive when I think—they would have had no tenderness for Molly!

They would have said, "You're not expecting me to mind that dog, are you?" Molly, who when something out in the street frightens her, runs in to where I'm standing, maybe at the sink or the cooker, and presses her thin body against my legs for protection. And I think for the first time—I let myself feel it—how did my mother and my father not care more for the small children around them? How did they not pick them up, not comfort them? How did my father strap his defenseless sons with his army belt? The dog gets her bits of stick and stone and arranges them between her paws so that she can guard them when she's asleep. These animals give me my first measure of what is owed to helpless beings. When I come home, the dog is sometimes waiting against the inside of the front door. The cat slides into the hallway when he hears the key, and cocks his little head up at me, and blinks his golden eyes, and wails righteously. As I come in I feel that the place has an air of pain, the way the home in Clontarf had. Mammy got the messages when she made her quick visit to the pub at lunchtime to steel herself for Daddy getting up in the afternoon. The children at home, powerless, had to wait for the messages. If I wanted to torment the dog and the cat, there would be nothing they could do.

The thing to do is: go out. That Christmas Day I did what my parents did on Bray Head and on Howth and in Inishowen when they were young and handsome and everything was going to be good. I sat on a headland and looked out at the world. The dog and I sat against a wall above Fanore and commanded, like conquerors, the prospect where this island ends in a shimmering haze of sea and sky. The turquoise shapes of Aran lay calm out on the horizon. There is always somewhere further to go. Each time I set off from Dublin in the direction of Naas or Maynooth or Swords—starting off to find something out, on my own, no one to worry about but myself, radio on, petrol in the tank, and money in my bag—that is the best there is. I'm conscious of it always, and full of inarticulate thanks. And I often wonder whether it is by accident or unconscious design that I'm doing exactly what my father did. He used to disappear every week to write his page for the back of *The Sunday Press* called "On the Road, with Terry O'Sullivan." And later, when he was doing "Dubliner's Diary," he didn't stick to Dublin then, either. He built in the events he made his milieu: the Rose of Tralee Festival, the Galway Oyster Festival, the Castlebar Song Festival. When honorary secretaries hurried forward across hotel lobbies to greet him with the utmost servility, snapping their fingers for Terry's bag to be taken, Terry's Paddy to be poured, it looked as if he needed to be bribed to be there. But for all his jaunty, impersonal tone, he was there out of love. He had an intemperate love for the fabric of Ireland. And I reap the harvest he sowed for me, in that as in other things.

There are things to see. I happened on an artwork that had been installed in a deserted house up a quiet country road between Belturbet and Clones, in that mysterious country where you don't know where the border is. The late-autumn day, when I was there, was silent and brown. The house had been left unlocked for whoever would come. With beating heart I pushed the door back and went in to the stillness of the rooms. The artist had covered the wall of the kitchen with shoes, worn shoes, and let blue dust accumulate in them. The marks on the shoes— the heels unevenly worn, the bulges toes had made, the cracks where foot and leather had accommodated each other—were pathetically faithful to the fleshiness and weight of the humans who had worn them. There were marks on the rough plaster walls and up the pitch-pine stairs, envelopes from old letters, and emigrants' luggage labels. A bedroom was hung with sheets like the sails of a ship. The sedgy fields outside, and rushes and willow scrub, and all the people gone . . . when I started the car going away a Bach tape came on, and I turned it off—quickly— because such elegance and attack isn't right. Not for this Ireland. But is it not wonderful that what was in the house was shaped and artful, not incoherent, like suffering? These sudden transformations happen all the time in Ireland; they are out there for me.

I'll go out to see such things. Or rather—things will make themselves seen. I might want to remember perfectly the stained glass at Chartres but actually remember, with perfection, the sticky surface of a table in a café near the station. I was in Dubrovnik on my own, in a season of torrential rain. I remember the look of the city well enough. But what I really saw, as I waited at a bus stop near a patch of waste ground, was—fully—the rain hit the puddle in front of me. I went up north of Toronto once, on a bus, to a small town. I spent a weekend there, on my way to somewhere else. I got a room in the usual deathly businessman's hotel—sealed picture windows, a dark and empty restaurant off the lobby echoing to the tinny sound of Muzak, a chlorine-smelling pool, with a salesman or two through the glass wall silently pumping at the Stairmaster. This was a town of two or three streets, a place which had served nineteenth-century settlers and prewar farmers and has no real role now. The weather was dull and cold. There was nothing for me to do. But I walked those streets of small houses in their grey winter shuttering, contented. The place had no significance. But it seemed to have meaning. And sometimes there is so much meaning that it gives an electric shock—like my first time in Athens, when I threw open the shutters of the hotel room and there, floating on the skyline, was the Parthenon, a complete surprise, golden against navy blue.

Perhaps places are for me what books were for my mother? They are altogether full of promise. They assuage some of the regret for all the lives I never had.

What is out there will be my partner. What I write about it will be the record of the relationship. Where I sat above the Atlantic, that Christmas afternoon, turns out to be almost an illustration. Behind me, up in the Burren, nothing knitted together. There's a prehistoric burial site. There's a village abandoned in the Famine. There's a tiny twelfth-century church. There's a holy well. There's a mound of shells near a cooking pit. Each thing is itself, discrete: near each other, and made from the same material, but never flowing into each other. That's how the life I have described here has been. There has been no steady accumulation; it has all been in moments.

But in front of me there is a vista: empty, but inexpressibly spacious. Between those two—landscape of stone and wide blue air—is where I am.

AFTERWORDS

That was how one Christmas Day ended. By the next Christmas that account of my life—written just for myself, as a sorting-out of myself—had changed everything. It itself had filled the emptiness that had seemed to be certainly waiting for me.

It is the twist in the tail of my story that the book was an instant best-seller. More than a best-seller—an emotional episode, somehow, in public life, in Ireland. It meant so much to some of its readers that when I went to bookshops to sign copies—a thing I had never in my life imagined doing—the event wasn't like something literary. It was as if we were already intimates, the people who came to the signings and myself. For a while, even, after I'd talked about the book on television, I had hardly been able to walk through Dublin between my house and the newspaper office, because people jumped out of cars to hug me, or stopped me to tell me about themselves, or ran after me to say that if I'd wait a minute they'd go into a shop and buy a copy, so I could write my name on it.

It lasted half a year, the disturbance surrounding publication. At last, the week before Easter, *Are You Somebody?* was replaced at the top of the best-seller list by someone else's book, after twenty weeks at number one. That day, Good Friday—the day I saw in the paper that it had begun to fade—I felt permitted to go back to private life. To going up and down the streets in my anonymous coat, looking at this or that. By then I accepted that something out of the ordinary had happened. My head-long account of myself had been reprinted over and over again. But what had changed for me hadn't to do with numbers sold. It was that what I had thought was merely personal had turned out to have meaning for other people. That was what I had to absorb.

Something had happened between this particular book and the people who sought it out. Even though, when I was sitting at the kitchen table putting words on the story, I had hardly thought of readers. I never had an image in my head of a person reading a book with my name on it. But the readers insisted on my seeing them. They offered me images of themselves in notes pushed through my door, in letters to me at the newspaper, in letters to my home, letters to me at the publishers. Hundreds and hundreds of letters. Yes, even one from a trekker's hut in Nepal. From kitchens and bedrooms and fireside chairs where men and women unknown to me had sat all night—in a sense with me—reading me. Letters came from Trinidad and Australia and China and Chicago. And from Rome, from a Jesuit I'd once known, who'd read my book in between hearing confessions.

I had my weekly afternoon of presence (CONFESSORE, DIREZIONE SPIRITUALE, says the notice over the desk) in the corner of the church of the biggest university in Europe. I used every free minute from the talkative young Italians (who do like to confess and explore faith and other areas especially with a foreigner) to continue reading your story.

Letters came from people who painted pictures I sometimes found it hard to look at:

I read a little of your book every night—it is part of my family ritual. My youngest daughter, five months old, goes to bed (on a good night) around 8:30 p.m. I curl her little body into mine, put the quilt over her so it is dark for her, breast-feed her, and I hold your book in my free hand and I read it.

I never envisaged such cherishing. When I called my memoir *Are You Somebody?* it was largely to preempt the hostile people who'd say, at my writing anything about myself at all, "Who does she think she is?" I never imagined awakening something a bit like love.

I do feel that somewhere within the meanings of the word "love" is the word for what happened. That Easter week, on the Good Friday, walking home from the centre of Dublin, I went into the old-fashioned Catholic church I pass every day, partly to pay my respects to Christianity and partly to try to draw a line under this part of my life. There's ample room for thinking in those huge churches, which are shells until they're filled by the faith of the people. A priest was putting a gaggle of small boys through a rehearsal of some ceremony: The candle gets carried out there, the book is fetched now, then you cross over behind the altar. . . . Ecclesiastical housework. Above their scurrying and whispering the tabernacle stood open. God was absent. In occlusion. Down in the underworld. But tomorrow He would rise again and irradiate the creation with His love. I tried to imagine it. Being loved. Someone knowing me, but loving me completely. Enough to die for me. I tried to be exact about what it was that had been offered to me by the people who'd written to me, if it wasn't a kind of love.

A formidable woman to whom I'd sent a copy of the book early on— I don't think she would have chosen to read it—had replied, "I have no doubt your account has given many people permission to feel good about themselves." I was chilled by such distancing. But I came to see that she was right. The telling out of pain, which is what a great many of the letters were, and the feeling of warmth towards me were part of one and the same impulse. This is typical:

I married and when he was thirty-three he had an affair, while I continued on because I had no money and I wanted the children to have two parents. I nursed him for five years with bone cancer and I am alone now. I passed you once, you wheeled a bike near Trinity, in a fur coat. I whispered, "I admire you so much."

This is exactly as the woman wrote it: the compressed life-story and the praise of me happen in the same breath. It seemed to me that I was being praised only because, though she recognised her own self-sacrifice, she was unable to praise herself for it. But then I'd think that maybe she'd read my journalism and seen me on television and really did admire me, and that it was I who could not accept praise.

Sometimes I could more clearly see that it was Ireland at the end of the twentieth century which was stirring. Hitherto silent voices within it were just on the brink of speaking out. I was just slightly ahead—just enough to be seen as a leader.

> I am a seventy-year-old grandmother from County Armagh who shared that reality or unreality of an alcoholic mother who was talented and beloved. . . . Keep up your brave heart. You have a mission to say what we the inarticulate or the hereditary hesitant feel and think.

I would pause, troubled, at a letter like this. She was projecting onto me the bravery it would take on her part to speak out. But it hadn't taken that bravery on my part. I wasn't knitted into society by grandchildren. In fact, as I had gone along, writing my memoir, two—I see now, contradictory—phrases repeated themselves in my head. One was, "Sure, no one will see it," and the other was, "What have I to lose, anyway?"

Male readers rang me, rather than wrote. They mostly rang anonymously, just to make contact, telling me nothing about themselves, though some did write long revelatory letters about alcoholism, sexual disappointment, loneliness within marriage, brutalities done to them in the home and at school. But mostly it was women who talked to me as if we were best friends. Very young women, like this one:

... An obscure sense of shame at being female—which I didn't even know was there—is dislodging itself in me. I wish I could give you something in return. All I have to offer is gratitude. P.S. Actually, I do have more to offer. Do you know all Alice Munro's books? If not, I would like to get you one, as a present.

But especially older women, like myself, who had lived long enough to turn around and ask, "What has my life amounted to?" The cadences of the letters were completely convincing.

I am not foolish enough to expect that passion should be burning bright after all the years but most of us would be satisfied with the odd interested question about ourselves, but the only ones we hear are, What is for the dinner? Is the same fucking dinner ready? Did the electricity bill come? Or if the children are coming home, not coming home, are they sick or well, making money or in debt—but never a word about me, just as a person, if I enjoyed or hated or loved or was interested in anything or anyone. No—I am not crying for myself—I am one of the lucky ones. I'm sorry I can't put my name to this—alas I have not got your honesty and I mustn't let the side down. I must go on belonging to that much-hyped bunch—the vast number of Ireland's strong happy marriages—onward Christian Soldier. Thanks, thanks again, Nuala, for that book. Everyone loves you.

"Everyone loves you." Each letter would have words like that. It was as if I were at my own funeral, and extravagant praise had been licensed. I often cried in those few months after the book came out. I couldn't get over the generosity within people, that had only been waiting for an opportunity to express itself. But I wasn't fundamentally moved. For me, it was as if someone was saying obviously pleasant things, but in a foreign language. In the church I remembered the exact words with which one letter had ended, and I all but wept again as I had when I read them.

"You are a good woman," the writer had said, "and God not only loves you but likes you." "Oh, no, He doesn't," I said to myself. "Where is He, if he does? Where is there love in *my* life?" The statues all around stayed mute.

It humiliates me to say it, but the truth is that I had lovers. That was what I would have called them, in their day. They would have said I was their lover. They must have read the book. But I got not even a friendly note from any former lover. I can't imagine a better proof of not being lovable. Not to have emerged with one single friend from all that ardour.

Yet I was immensely the better for what had happened. I had a new vitality, even if my range was still very narrow, and my emotions still revolved around self-pity. My old self-pity—I could feel it, as I took stock—had been transformed by the responses it evoked. It had become something valuable. It spoke so authentically to strangers that it had become a medium, carrying experience between them and me. There was so much they hadn't felt able to mourn until they saw me mourning for myself. Between us, we might even put mourning away. There was nothing, I felt as I sat in my pew, that people could say that I could not, from now on, take. I could even take silence.

I answered every letter. Sometimes I arranged to meet people, when words failed me. I met an elderly man who had taken on all the sadnesses of his brothers and sisters, raised like him in orphanages after their mother died young. Every sentence of his long letter shook with pain. There was a litany of wasted lives, heartbreaking deaths:

And once a fortnight I visit another sister, who was a lovely girl possessed of a beautiful singing voice when she was young. When aged about twenty she was in and out of various psychiatric hospitals before going to London. It was the last place for an innocent girl like her, and I believe she was seduced there by an older Irishman. This probably had the effect of pushing her over the brink. My father and I went over and brought her home. For over fifteen years she has been in the high-security wing of a mental hospital, hopelessly, frighteningly, deranged. On the surface my visits serve little purpose and certainly do me no good. But she once said, "You're the only one I have," and so I keep going and wishing that death might come quickly to give her that peace she never found in life.

In the pub where we met for a coffee, this precise and dapper man had these things well under control. We pushed each subject out towards the abstract. We talked about developments in the care of the mentally ill in Ireland, for example, as opposed to his own sick sister. We talked about his dog and my dog. People can't talk as they can write. The same reticence that keeps them lonely keeps them upright.

I answered letters even when I didn't know what to say. A mother whose children were growing up and away and whose friend and—first woman—lover had left her, wrote:

After a shower the towel falls away and feeling soft and warm I stroke my body. Until, that is, my eyes meet mine in the mirror and my heart feels heavy. Is this going to be enough? Or maybe it all settles? Hopefully?

How could I answer that? I wrote to her and said, "Maybe something marvellous will happen."

A man wrote to me from a room where he'd been sitting up all night, gladdened for the proof that he was not quite alone when a light would come on in a neighbour's house.

My long-term lady friend, who I trusted and lived for, some time ago simply said, "The dream is over. It's never going to be."

Trust, sincerity, and sexual emotions are linked together. How can I re-establish my reason for existing?

I don't know how. I wrote to him, too, to say that something wonderful might happen. Though it's not happening to me, I said to myself. Then one day I realised that it was: that these floods of trusting letters were it. They were the something wonderful.

But that didn't stop them hurting. A woman who had spent Christmas entirely alone wrote to me:

I had a relationship for four years, begun at thirty. It was a marvellous chance for me. He is married, with children, very much in love with his family and for some strange reason loved me too for some years. I never see him now, love him to bits, and think about him regularly. I'm at the stage, though, where I'm fairly happy most days. I have always had poor health. I depend on blood transfusions. I know I'm lucky really. Like your woman in *Madison County*, having had the experience of true love I can put up with anything.

I don't know how to console for such losses. And as for the bitter pain of sexual loneliness, humans seem to have been left by their gods to deal with that by themselves. Nothing in the church I was sitting in could help me to help a woman—a woman I knew slightly, once a famous beauty—who had written to me about a reflection, in my book, on making love:

This morning I got stuck again at your sentence beginning, "The remembered fluency with another person. . . ." Well, Nuala, I never had it, ever. Always, and for as long as I can remember, I solitarily and anxiously circle around behind my barriers and ramparts of books and house-improvement projects and 24-hour radio. I am afraid to look in mirrors in case I see my father, madness, or a void.

The stories told to me in the letters have moved in with me. They were handed to me, and I hold them, even though I'm as helpless to reach out and change them as my readers are helpless to make my life other than what it is. An old man wrote to me:

> I have first-hand experience of dealing with depression because my wife has suffered from it for about fifty years. Fortunately she has kept clear of alcohol but I have experience of two suicide attempts and one car crash.

I want to say to him that I grieve for the two of them.

A young mother wrote to me:

> I watch *Upstairs Downstairs* and *Dallas* before the children come home from school and as I watch the actresses and actors in them go for the bottle whenever they return to the house, I too feel like a drink. It is a temptation. My mother used to succeed in making several trips to the bar during the evening. Now, Nuala, everybody says I'm the image of her. I can see it myself when I look in the mirror. I like a little sherry and have now progressed to a gin and tonic.

I want to say I fear for her.

I want to say "I'm glad you fled to America" to an Irishwoman who wrote to me from there:

> My mother had ten children, nine males and one female (me), and survived the squalid darkness of rural Ireland in the forties with a husband who "never cracked a match to light a candle or warmed a bottle for any of you"—her words, oft-quoted, and acknowledged by him.

And to another who also wrote from there:

> My youngest sister died at age eighteen from leukaemia and of
> the eight remaining children seven are alcoholic and a number are
> also drug dependant as well. All those absolutely beautiful babies
> my mother had (and we were all beautiful to look at) were sys-
> tematically annihilated emotionally by their abusive father. I
> spent years being very angry at my mother because she didn't
> save us, but now I realise that she didn't really have any choice but
> to stay with him. On one occasion she told the priest of the abuse
> and he advised her to go back to him. When she did leave, he to-
> tally cut her off financially. What he wanted in the following or-
> der were 1) his sex, 2) his warm meal on the table when he walked
> in, 3) his warm fire. All the good she did as a mother was totally
> obliterated by him, by his abuse, his drunkenness, his horrible
> anger.

I hadn't intended dropping into the church to be of any significance—not the religious side of it. It was just a place to sit down and
think. If the pubs had been open I would have gone in to a quiet morning pub. But I remembered the letters when I looked around, on Good
Friday, and saw the purple cloths they cover the images with, during
Holy Week, to remind us of Christ's Passion. What about the ordinary
passion of people! I thought. Look how much ordinary men and women
know about being crucified! No wonder we strain ourselves to believe
that there is a God, who loves us.

One of my readers sent me part of a long poem. She had written it out
on a Good Luck card. I found a phone number for her and rang her
within minutes, to ask for the whole poem. She sent it that day, and she
might as well have sent me gold. The poem is called "In the Wake of
Home," by Adrienne Rich. Part of it talks about:

The family coil   so twisted, tight and loose
anyone trying to leave
has to strafe the field
burn the premises down

The home houses
mirages   memory fogs the kitchen panes
the rush-hour traffic outside
has the same old ebb and flow
Out on the darkening block
somebody calls you home
night after night   then never again
Useless for you to know
they tried to do what they could
before they left for good. . . .

The poem seemed to rise above everything else that was said to me, as if it told the truth about certain childhoods and could show me a way of accepting mine. Because I was still looking for my own parents. And among the letters that came were a few precious ones that led me back to them, brought definition to them, as if photos of them had been thrown into a developing tank and were swimming up to the surface with random bits of their blurry images—here an elbow, there a strap on a shoe—taking on shape.

I never could imagine, for instance, my mother as a child. She'd cut all that off, herself. I didn't even know her name then was Caitlin. My father called her Katherine. But I got some letters. A woman who'd been at primary school with her wrote:

> I knew your mother and loved her. She was a leader and got
> us into all kinds of rows. Caitlin wrote a play for Christmas
> about a poor craythur from the country looking for Woolworth's

cafeteria—the first one in the city. I'm talking about the 1930s. I remember how we fell around laughing, and of course she was the culchie and did it to perfection, makeup and all. We would all have been about twelve, that was it. I was given a present of your book but I was so sad for your Mam I couldn't read it.

Then a very elderly nun wrote. She'd been Mammy's friend at her next school, the boarding-school in Donegal. I've written about the tragedy of my mother having a crush there on an older girl, a girl in the sixth year. I'd known that Mammy had been expelled because of her, and that the expulsion was in some way the trauma of her life. The nun sent a sixty-four-year-old photo of a girl—my mother—in her school uniform, and I hardly knew how to look at it. It was the only photo of my mother as a girl that I had ever seen. This nun had begun reading my book "over a sandwich and a cup of coffee in a café. Hungry as I was, I had to leave the sandwich and head for the privacy of the car—I felt so sad." Imagine—two old women, still liking my mother enough to be sad at what became of her!

The nun told me my mother was frighteningly intense.

None of my *terra firma* attitudes sufficed to keep Caitlin's passions on an even keel once she became "struck" on her sixth-year beauty! You can imagine how Caitlin's imagination ran riot when she had pen and paper to hand! A nun found a laundry bag full of notes at the foot of Caitlin's bed. It is my firm belief that it was on these masterpieces that judgement was passed. The trial went on for the whole of Lent. The Sixth-Year and Caitlin were sent home. Caitlin ran away *en route* home and was found in Belfast. I felt heartbroken over your mother. Even with hindsight, we were innocent, naïve teenagers—crazily romantic but no more.

I don't remember Mammy mentioning Belfast. And she wouldn't have forgotten. Never.

Then one evening, not long after I got these letters, I played back a phone message when I came home. The voice was that of another old lady, uncertain and slow—not used to leaving messages, perhaps. "Hello? Hello?" the voice said. "Is that Nuala's house? I want to talk to Nuala. I was a Sixth-Year when your mother was at school—the one she got into trouble about. I very much want to meet you and talk because—" I hadn't dared ask this woman, the one time I met her at a reception in Dublin, what had really happened. But then the phone message ran out! The beep came. She hadn't left a phone number or address, and I don't know her name.

But it wasn't the long-ago story that moved me most. It was praise for my mother when she was the woman I knew myself, the only praise that in all my life I ever heard said of her.

Over twenty years ago, [a letter from a woman began], I worked in Howth library. During that time I met your mother. I watched your mother come in from the car loaded down with books—yes, I'd realise that she had a problem with drink, but more importantly this was a lady. She talked to me as if I were an equal— "You should read that one, it's enjoyable; hated that one, no plot." For me your mother was someone who shared my passion for books. When she said "I read that one again—I couldn't do without a read," I knew exactly what she meant. I never thought of her as a mother/wife/alcoholic—she was a reader. Her husky voice was never coarse. Why I remember her so clearly I don't know.

"This was a lady." Imagine that. It was we—the family—who defined her "mother/wife/alcoholic."

And my father. . . . Another evening I was at home and answered the phone to a tentative, flustered voice. It took awhile for this woman to say what she needed to say. She had been for some years, it turned out, the counsellor of my father's most important mistress, Carmel. Carmel was

201

a terribly troubled person, apparently, and a driver in a big car used to take her, regularly, to this counsellor's house.

He never lent his car to send Mammy to a counsellor, I was thinking bitterly, when I realised what the woman on the phone was saying. "Did you know Carmel killed herself?" she was saying.

No. I did not know that Carmel killed herself. I gathered myself to ask, "Did she kill herself before or after my father died himself?" "Oh, before. She killed herself because of your father. I've never known a woman so terrified of being left. An overdose, I believe it was. Her son found her in the morning." That must have been close to the end of the pas de trois.

A man famous in the public relations business—the kind of person my father knew and never dropped his guard with—wrote me a shocked letter. It began:

I knew your father. I knew your mother. I knew your father's friend Frank Finn. I knew Carmel. Now I know I knew nothing. . . . One day—in the late '70s—your father turned up unexpectedly at the Irish Open Golf in Portmarnock and even though extremely busy I dropped everything to be with him. His agenda was different. It was Frank Finn. He cried and talked and cried some more. He told me of his praying for Frank and of his visits to the chapel that had replaced the Red Bank restaurant. He told me he himself was ill. In a word he was scared and I pitied him. Little did I know then or until this week what a tortured soul he must have been.

Yes, yes, I want to say. The poor, solitary man. My heart fills with pity for him. Then the pity retreats when I open another letter. It is from a woman who was at school with my youngest sister—a child who had no one to watch out for her except my father, because my mother was too drunk and sick to count. "Our teacher was an embittered woman," one part of the letter said, and the punishments she dished out to little scraps, which is what we were at the time, were terrible. My mother gave me lunch for your sister as she rarely had any of her own. I remember the day your little sister came to school with no pants on. We were all astonished at this, and nervous giggles and laughter drew the teacher's attention. Instead of helping or comforting your sister, she slapped the legs off her and told her to "Go home. The party might still be going on."

Even now, after time to absorb it, I am rocked by that teacher's cruelty. And her own unhappiness. What lascivious images must she have had of the "party" in my little sister's sad home? But there was a context, to the teacher and to all the others and to ourselves, the O'Faolains. There was an Ireland—a whole society—that in those times allowed such things.

What that Ireland was like came to be very precisely symbolised for me. Our family, when we were still all at home, lived in a house on the seafront in Clontarf. It was one of a line of houses, facing the sea across a road and a thin strip of grassed promenade. It was a dull place. But during winter storms, sometimes, great waves curved themselves hugely across the grass and smashed onto the road. There's a photo a newspaper took of one particularly dramatic stormy day there. My sister in London has a blowup of it on her wall. Foamy, immensely powerful waves rear up in the foreground, and the houses of ourselves and our neighbours seem to cower behind them. The atmosphere inside the houses, it turns out, could be as menacing.

Even now, it astonishes me and even frightens me that I got letters from not one but two women who as girls lived within sight of our house, one to the right of us, one to the left, though they didn't know each other. "I hated Clontarf, and still do," one of the letters said.

We often were starving in that dreadful house on the Clontarf Road, facing the cinder-strewn grey strip that was then being reclaimed to make the prom. On the surface great respectability was kept up—that was the worst of it—keeping up appearances.

And the other letter, from twenty or thirty doors away on that one road, said:

> Whereas you thought you saw wealth in my home I can say I often longed for the educational richness you had in your parents. My home had all the outward signs of "everything." Any attempt to call for help or disclose the cruelty both physical and emotional was negated by adults and teachers alike. Today my father would simply have been jailed for his cruelty to his children.

What were the forces at work in Ireland then?

The Adrienne Rich poem describes a happy childhood:

> *You sleep in a room with bluegreen curtains*
> *posters   a pile of animals on the bed*
> *A woman and a man who love you*
> *and each other   slip the door ajar*
> *you are almost asleep   they crouch in turn*
> *to stroke your hair   you never wake*
>
> *This happens every night for years*
> *This never happened.*

Those girls in Clontarf did not belong to happy homes in childhood, and neither did I, and neither did my own mother. And many, many millions more. But what the poem does is to offer unhappy children somewhere to belong. It puts us, who happen to be Irish and women, into a wider context. And there, we belong. There, we find we are speaking a mother tongue.

What if I told you your home
is this continent of the homeless
of children sold   taken by force
driven from their mothers' land
killed by their mothers to save from capture
—this continent of changed names and mixed-up blood
of languages tabooed
diasporas unrecorded
undocumented refugees
underground railroads   trails of tears
What if I tell you your home
is this planet of warworn children
women and children standing in line or milling
endlessly calling each others' names
What if I tell you, you are not different
it's the family albums that lie
—will any of this comfort you
and how should this comfort you?

A church sounds like a genteel place to sit. I must have looked like the usual kind of solitary worshipper, in the church on Good Friday: a middle-aged woman with shopping. But there's nothing genteel about the life inside me. In there, it is as if I live in a condition of turbulence, always moving between opposites—well-being and sadness, delight and dullness, acceptance and restless regret. Not a day had passed since the book came out that other people hadn't shown me that their lives, too, however static they may look, are on the move all the time. And all the images around me in the church spoke of the same magnetic poles. Our Lady of Perpetual Succour opened her embracing arms in love; Christ was contorted on His cross in pain.

I was holding inside myself the reverberations of a transaction between love and pain. Part of it had come about because of daring to write a memoir. I'd called the book *Are You Somebody?* But I had wanted for a long time to call it *Personal Ad*. It did confess. Especially it confessed—evasively, far too prettily—to sexual yearnings I could not assuage. Once responses began to flood in I began to hope even for that. Maybe someone who'd read it would come for me and change everything? But nothing happened. I'd go out, and there would be praise and affection and even drama: a person standing in front of me, for instance, with tears running down her face, saying, "Thank you for what you wrote. Thank you. Thank you." And I would come home to my quiet room. I'd say to the cat and the dog, "Any Princes or Princesses Charming come down the chimney while I was out? No? Thought as much."

And then a man sought me out. He said he'd read the book. I met him for a drink on the way home one evening. He didn't have a copy of the book, and I didn't mention it. On the way out of the pub, in the dark corridor, he came up behind me and suddenly took command of my head and tilted it back and began to pull at my lips with his, and when I put my hand up to feel his face—the first strange, living face that I had touched in years—he caught the side of my hand in his mouth and chewed on it, as if he were ravenous to eat me. And with that hint of being desired, I was an alpine range to which hot spring had come. I leafed and blossomed and sprouted meadows of silky grass. I hummed with intense life. He walked beside me to the taxi rank, and the quiet things he said were wonderful promises about the knowing each other there was going to be. That short encounter was the version of love that came into my life.

As for pain: That very night they rang from London to say that my brother Don had been found dead in his room. I fell to the floor beside the phone, weak with sorrow, and I called the little dog and held her to me. Our Don, who—I had never known, till I got his reply when I wrote to him about this book—used to hide in the chest of drawers when he heard Daddy hitting Mammy. Don, who went in to the British army to survive and couldn't survive coming out of it. He had died of drink. And self-starvation. And—of sadness. He had been in touch, over the last few months, with my sister Deirdre in Dublin, whom we all love and trust. Deirdre knew he was drinking himself to death and she was trying to get some of the funny little essays he used to write out of him, so as to get them published, so as to maybe make him want to live. One was accepted—about the pig he looked after for our grandaunts in Athlone, and how the pig ate the new concrete Don tried to mend its sty with, and how then the pig was sold and he was sure it would make concrete rashers. It came out in *Ireland's Own* the very week he died. He never saw it.

Deirdre showed me his last letter to her, the one after which there would be no more:

Nuala sent me *Are You Somebody?* It's surprising that a sister and a brother can view the same father in such different lights. Odd. Nuala's book was not written for the likes of me. An intellectual book way over my head, except for when she went for the jugular. But I never read Baudelaire or Flaubert or drank in McDaid's. I do know a lot of the characters who appear. Rob—how about the biggest arty-farty intellectual there is? Thirty years ago he found me "coarse and loud." What did the arsehole expect from me? I'm trying to impress my genius sister. They speak of classics, Italian tints, French impressionists: and I'm trying to learn the semi-automatic rifle, the heavy machine-gun, drill, fieldcraft, and an Understanding of Discipline. I shall be writing to thank her for the book but in due course as I haven't figured out at all how to go about writing something that makes me doltish.

Does he mean the book made him feel a dolt? Or that the book made him out to *be* a dolt? I'll never know. Oh, if I could speak to him—to tell him I never, never, thought of him as a dolt! But I will never speak to him. He did try to ring me not long before he died. He was in a telephone box somewhere. His money ran out before he said anything much but "hello." You don't believe it, about your family, that the discussion is over, for ever. It wasn't that I saw him often, or communicated with him much. But that was just a phase! Nothing was at all concluded. Someday there would have been something further.

I don't have to live with just that smarting word, "dolt." Deirdre wouldn't have shown me the letter if that was all there was. She is kind. Don was kind, in the first place, because he went on to tell this story:

When I decided I couldn't do another winter on London's streets, nor face going home again in rags to Father's ridicule, I joined the British Army. As far as I was concerned, I didn't have a family, no one knew where I was, and couldn't give a hoot if they did. A nice recruiting sergeant gave me £1 expenses and a railway warrant to Sutton Coldfield. Thirteen weeks on they have turned me from a gauche, naïve, totally lost innocent into exactly the same, but I can march around the square to a band and drums, with a rifle with bayonets fixed. No one knew I was "Passing Out," and anyway, I was in the middle of bloody nowhere. Parade over. Meet your folks in the shed over there. Nuala. A little wave. I'm too shocked and stunned to even stutter properly. She had come all that way from her work in London to spend five minutes with me, as she had to get back. I was eighteen years old then and I am still as moved by her kindness if not more so, now I'm fifty-one. Funny old world.

I remember very well that long journey to Sutton Coldfield. I had a good record with Don when he was a neglected boy. That's what got me through his death. Because I didn't have any kind of record with him when he was a man. But so did the secret excitement of the man I'd met get me through. My veins ran hot; the frost of sadness couldn't settle on them. He had said, "I'll give you a ring this evening, pet," when we parted, but he hadn't rung. He still hadn't rung when I had to go to London a few days later, to say goodbye to Don's body. But I was still waiting. I hadn't lost hope.

Hope was a transgression. I was meant to feel nothing but grief, all through the obsequies for Don. I would have been ashamed if anyone knew how often I retreated from them to go over in my mind the meeting with the man and what he'd said about the future. But Don didn't need helping anymore. I did. I went to London and got a bus to the undertakers in Camden Town and saw my brother's yellow-grey face, and his hands folded across his thin body, in the coffin lined with polyester satin. He hadn't eaten for months before he died. No one could make him eat: his daughters, his neighbours, his friends. His lips were still obstinate. He would never say anything to anyone for all eternity. My jokey brother, who used to look like Tony Curtis. I saw black rot in his fingertips. I never saw anything in my life as—as indifferent to me and all the living, as that blackness. His body wasn't even pretending to carry a person anymore. What or where Don was, was the most unanswerable question. I never heard silence like there was in the little room with his body in it. I never saw anything more immobile than Don in that still place.

His long-estranged wife and the son who had stayed with her came over from Dublin to the cremation, in a fake-Gothic chapel in a graveyard, in a London suburb. There was the sad side of things; there was also the other side. Don's daughters and my London sister, for instance, put together a tape of music he'd liked, for the service of cremation, and they put it together with love. They put in the sweetness of John Lennon singing "In My Life," and they put in "The Daughter of the Regiment" because it is funny and Don liked funniness, and they chose the exuberant aria where Pavarotti sings a sequence of high Cs because Don enjoyed showing off, too. I had scarcely known this man they evoked so fondly. But in the crematorium chapel the boy I did know, inside the thin, greying man, slipped away—that awful, soundless slide of the coffin—when Elvis was singing on the tape the spiritual in the middle of "American Trilogy":

> *Hush little baby, don't you cry,*
> *You know your daddy's bound to die.*
> *All my trials, Lord,*
> *Soon be over. . . .*

209

The congregation, small as it was, had every kind of person in it, in every kind of condition. Just like Don's life. Some people smelled of drink; some were impeccable. The British army was represented. There was a Union Jack on his coffin, yet Don's name was O'Faolain. A bugler sounded the Last Post. Heartbreak made audible. "Did you know your brother played golf with the Governor of the Falklands?" some major said to me in the pub afterwards. Little children—the children of nieces and nephews—ran around between the chairs and tables of the pub. They were already much happier than we had been, even when we were as small as they.

The following day we went to my sister's flat and we played the Elvis trilogy loudly and more loudly. "Glory, glory, hallelujah!" we roared. I had a few humorous letters Don had sent me long ago when he was a new soldier. I read them out. But no one was very interested in that far back. I was stuck in the past, just myself, and my caricature of him. I remembered his desperate face when I bumped into him one winter's evening in an alleyway off Eden Quay, when he was about twelve, and he'd been missing for a while, living rough after some fight at home. I see that face now, half turning up to me, half turning to run away. He was tired out, and he was only a child! I was surprised all the time in the flat by the others' reminiscences of a man, the Don recently dead. A Don who was a father and a grandfather. Loved. I am a stranger to these loves my brothers and sisters know with the families they started themselves. I'm still back at the first family. The mourners had stood around outside the chapel after the cremation service. I might have picked out my dear brothers and sisters by their awkwardness. None of us was ever held, for pleasure, by my mother, and my father wouldn't have held a small body, even for a photographer. The next generation touch each other lavishly.

A daughter read out a few pieces Don had written towards the end. He had been sitting with his duvet around him for seven years. Sometimes he couldn't keep his mind dead with vodka and he'd write something, with a ball-point pen, on a lined pad, just for himself. He wrote a piece about incest. "Why not keep it in the family?" this would-be witty piece ended. The things sex involves might have saved Don, and he knew it. But he couldn't move from the neighbourhood inside him. He had to stay with the familiar drinking. He knew his way blindfold around that. "I recommend celibacy," he'd said to his daughter. "I haven't had sex for years and I don't miss it." He meant the opposite. Those boasts always mean the opposite.

When I thought of him in his chair I saw Mammy with him, as if her shadow sat in the chair with him and raised his bottle to his glass with him and read his book with him. But he was conscious of his dying as she never was. A Yevtushenko poem was near him when he did die. Technically he was drunk when he died. But what does "drunk" mean when you say it about someone as sure of his purposes as Don was? The poem tells us what was in his head: the cathedral he had made there, the hushed, arched place where he balanced consciousness against the dissolution of consciousness. It begins:

> *Inside me the season is autumn,*
> *the chill is in me, you can see through me,*
> *and I am sad, but not altogether cheerless,*
> *and filled with humility and goodness.*
>
> *But if I rage sometimes,*
> *then I am the one whose rage is shedding my leaves. . . .*

And in the middle it says:

> *Something has apparently happened to me*
> *And I am relying on nothing but silence,*
> *When the leaves laying themselves one on another*
> *Inaudibly become the earth.*

Don's body became ashes. After I came back to Dublin my own became ashy to me. It was a month before the man who'd said he wanted to know me rang me up. I didn't utter any of the reproaches I'd practised. He said he'd be around with a pizza and a bottle of wine. The hours passed. Growing incredulity is meant to be comic. Mine wasn't comic. The next day was my birthday. He never turned up and he never rang.

What does it matter? Isn't death coming up behind us, my brothers and sisters and myself? Aren't we like children playing O'Grady Says? Whoever was playing O'Grady shouted orders at the line of children creeping up behind him. If O'Grady caught you moving when he whirled around—if you hadn't frozen into a statue quickly enough, on the spot—O'Grady called you "out." Death caught Don out. One of the rest of us will be caught out next. The ground is fissuring beneath our feet. Since the phone rang to tell me Don was dead, I'm afraid of what the phone will say next.

That's why the man matters. Because death is coming. That's why. Because I want to live. When I was in the church on Good Friday going over in my mind what the publication of the book had meant, I tried to sort the important things out. I was full of anger about Don. I was raw about the man. But there were all the people who'd sent me their love, hundreds of them. Given it freely, and given it to someone they knew, if only by my own description. Is that what I must settle for, then? I thought. That I can have love—but the love of people I can't see or touch?

It seems to me that the Adrienne Rich poem says that there are wounds that don't heal.

> *Any time you go back*
> *the familiar underpulse*
> *will start its throbbing: HOME, HOME!*
> *and the hole torn and patched over*
> *will gape unseen again.*

My sister said, "Don's daughters want his ashes brought back to Ireland and put in Mammy and Daddy's grave." "They *what?*" I said.

"Why would they put him in with his murderers?" Then after a while I said, "Sure, why not? If there is any heaven they're all young again, the three of them, and full of hope again, and they don't dream of ever harming each other." My sister said, "He had books and music at the end, you know. He got that from them. That's not nothing." I said, "It is nothing. Compared with what you want to get from your father and mother." But by the time I sat in the church on Good Friday—Don had been dead for two months—I could think, without being too hurt for him or any of the rest of us, "In heaven, Mammy and Daddy will even want his company."

In the next church along the street there is a shrine to St. Valentine. Japanese newlyweds go to it on their honeymoons. I go to it. I've prayed for love. If I can't receive it, at least to give it. And if I can't have it at all, at least to let others have it. I see the line of stain running through our family. Like rust, gradually dribbling further and further down a wall. My mother didn't want us. She hadn't felt wanted herself. The poem doesn't find a way out of that.

> *The child's soul musters strength*
> *where the holes were torn*
> *but there are no miracles:*
> *even children become exhausted*
> *And how shall they comfort each other*
> *who have come young to grief?*
> *Who will number the grains of loss*
> *and what would comfort be?*

It wasn't marriage that did her in. She wanted him. It was motherhood. It was us. But we didn't make her suffer. It was love and passion that made her suffer. It was that that undermined them all: my mother, and my father, and Carmel. There was a degree of pain in their dealings with love and passion that, all unexpectedly, I realised I was coming to terms with, through my book. Not through writing it but through publishing it. It was the warmth the book met that had made me strong.

And, more mysteriously, made them strong, in my thinking about them. Worthy—I began to see—of many better things than pity, even when I brought to mind memories that had once seemed to me impossibly sad. Mammy asked me to meet her, once, in a pub in the centre of Dublin. That kind of memory. I was about eighteen, and I was living in a bed-sitter. She'd found a letter from Carmel in my father's coat pocket. Carmel was in England. "My breasts have got bigger," a sentence in the letter said. "You'll see when I get back." We sat side by side looking at the letter on the smeary table. What could my mother do? There was nothing she could do.

Not long after that, she agreed to go into a psychiatric hospital for her drinking. He and his car weren't around. I brought her, in a taxi. But we didn't have the money for the taxi. I got out, and had it wait outside a pawnshop in Marlborough Street, and pawned her wedding ring, to pay for the taxi. That symbol of their marriage was the only thing she had worth a few pounds. But at least she died quickly. Think of Carmel—so unhappy that she left her son to find her body. Think of my father—not able to talk to either woman or talk about either woman. Think of his privacy invaded when Mammy and I looked at the intimacies in his letter. Think that what he would have wanted to believe about himself was often made a mockery of by his appetites.

"But I'd do the same, myself!" I burst out that day in the church. "I'd make the choices those three did!" There's nothing I wouldn't stop at in the pursuit of even a parody of love. "Forgive them," I heard myself saying to myself, "the same way you forgive yourself, for the same reasons you forgive yourself."

And with that—a tiny moment but a true one—something inside me, that had been agitated for as long as I could remember, went quiet for the first time. I didn't feel lightened, as people in novels do. But I thought, Why didn't I see that before? That they were only ordinary, too.

I heard the voices of the priest and the children practising—"Slowly, now, boys and girls! Slowly!"—how to process up the aisle. When they'd all arrived at the altar in stately enough fashion he said they could go, and they raced past me and out the big doors, which swished and banged with their escape, and then the whole church was silent and empty, except for me. I got ready to leave. I'm going back to private life now, I said to myself. The book thing is over. It hadn't ended where I ended it. The story wasn't over in the snow on a hillside above the Atlantic. Isn't that extraordinary? I wasn't in charge. I controlled nothing. I didn't know that for more people than I could imagine this account of one unregarded life would be a thing that would flower and flower. No more than I knew that Don was sitting quietly in his chair, and that in the end the quiet would turn into stiffness, and he would have gone away.

What can I do but take my chances? I was thinking incoherently, coming out of the chapel into the midday light. And what else can I do? Look after my teeth, listen to all the music I can, and keep going. Keep working on my escape tunnels out of the past. Keep hoping to break through to the here-and-now. To be just myself, like the cat, which is so perfectly and unself-consciously a cat and does not know it will perish. What can I do, when everything is so various and so beyond me, but cling on, and thank the God I don't believe in for the miracles showered on me?